CELLS, TISSUES
& ORGANS

THE SCIENCE OF THE HUMAN BODY

BODY SYSTEMS

CELLS, TISSUES & ORGANS

DISEASES

EPIDEMICS & PANDEMICS

GENES & GENETICS

IMMUNOLOGY

MASON CREST
450 Parkway Drive, Suite D, Broomall, Pennsylvania 19008
(866) MCP-BOOK (toll-free)

James Shoals

First printing
9 8 7 6 5 4 3 2 1

ISBN (hardback) 978-1-4222-4193-6
ISBN (series) 978-1-4222-4191-2
ISBN (ebook) 978-1-4222-7612-9

Cataloging-in-Publication Data on file with the Library of Congress

Developed and Produced by National Highlights Inc.
Interior and cover design: Torque Advertising + Design
Production: Michelle Luke

THE SCIENCE OF THE HUMAN BODY

CELLS, TISSUES & ORGANS

JAMES SHOALS

MASON CREST

KEY ICONS TO LOOK FOR:

 Words to Understand: These words with their easy-to-understand definitions will increase the reader's understanding of the text while building vocabulary skills.

 Sidebars: This boxed material within the main text allows readers to build knowledge, gain insights, explore possibilities, and broaden their perspectives by weaving together additional information to provide realistic and holistic perspectives.

 Educational videos: Readers can view videos by scanning our QR codes, providing them with additional educational content to supplement the text. Examples include news coverage, moments in history, speeches, iconic sports moments, and much more!

 Text-Dependent Questions: These questions send the reader back to the text for more careful attention to the evidence presented there.

 Research Projects: Readers are pointed toward areas of further inquiry connected to each chapter. Suggestions are provided for projects that encourage deeper research and analysis.

QR CODES AND LINKS TO THIRD-PARTY CONTENT

CONTENTS

Cells.. 6
Tissues 10
Blood 14
Bones 17
Tendons, Ligaments, & Cartilage 21
Brain 24
Heart 27
Lungs 30
Kidneys 33
Stomach 37
Liver 40
Eye 43
Ear 46
Nose 49
Tongue 52
Skin 55
Intestines 58
Neurons 61
Spinal Cord 64
Donation & Transplantation 67
Artificial Limbs 71
Text-Dependent Questions 74
Research Projects 76
Further Reading 77
Internet Resources 77
Index 78

CELLS

Cells are the building blocks of life. They are of different shapes and sizes, and perform a variety of functions. In some organisms, cells have simple structures, but cells in animals and plants are complex. They have many **organelles** and a nucleus.

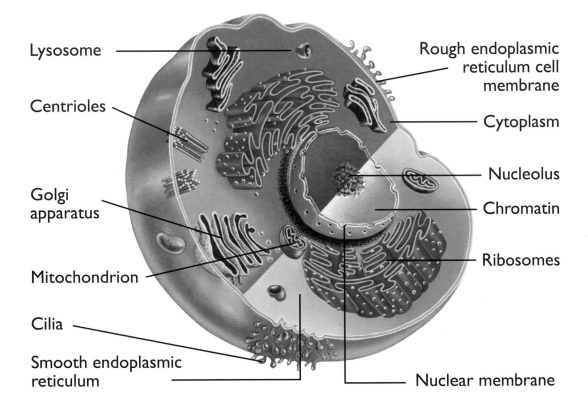

Lysosome

Centrioles

Golgi apparatus

Mitochondrion

Cilia

Smooth endoplasmic reticulum

Rough endoplasmic reticulum cell membrane

Cytoplasm

Nucleolus

Chromatin

Ribosomes

Nuclear membrane

WORDS TO UNDERSTAND

botanist: a person who studies about plants and their life cycle.

organelles: specialized structures within a cell.

physiologist: a person who studies about living things and their behavior.

The Cell Theory

After the invention of the microscope, many groundbreaking discoveries were made in the field of life sciences. Robert Hooke discovered the cell in 1665. In 1674, Antonie Van Leeuwenhoek described the first single-celled organism, bacterium. In 1678, Leeuwenhoek reported the observation of "little animals," or protozoa, in a water sample. In 1838, Matthias Jakob Schleiden, a German **botanist** who used a microscope to study plants, stated that all the parts of plants are composed of cells. When Schleiden mentioned his observation to his **physiologist** friend Theodor Schwann, Schwann realized that he had seen a similar structure in animals. Together, they put forth what is now known as the cell theory. It states that:

- every living organism is made of cells.
- the cell is the basic unit of life.
- all cells arise from preexisting cells.

Robert Hooke

Characteristics of Cells

- Every cell has its own organs called organelles.
- All cells can grow, divide, and die.
- Cells have genetic material that stores information.

Types of Cells

Cells are of differing sizes and shapes, and they perform varied functions. However, the basic components of all cells are the same. Each body part is made up of a specific type of cell depending on the functions it performs. Bone cells are rigid and help shape our bodies, while red blood cells are flexible and carry oxygenated blood to various organs. Nerve cells are long, thin, and narrow, whereas muscle cells are rod-shaped.

Structure of a Human Cell

Cell membrane
The boundary of a cell

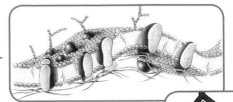

Cytoskeleton
The internal framework of a cell

Cytoplasm
The jelly-like material
inside the cell

Nucleus
The control center of a cell

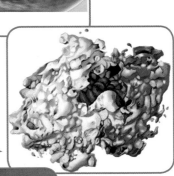

Chromosomes
Genetic material that
stores information

Mitochondria
Produces energy from food

Ribosomes
Help in making proteins

Golgi complex
Stores protein and releases
it when needed

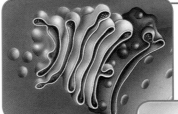

Lysosome
Digests food

Endoplasmic reticulum
Helps transport protein
to the cell

Cell Division

Cells divide every day, every hour, and every second of our lives. The process of cell division is called mitosis. When a cell divides, it produces cyclins, proteins that helps cells in mitosis. Cells follow a routine regarding when to take food in, when to divide, and when to stop working or die. The process of the programmed death of cells is called apoptosis. This pattern is known as the "cell cycle."

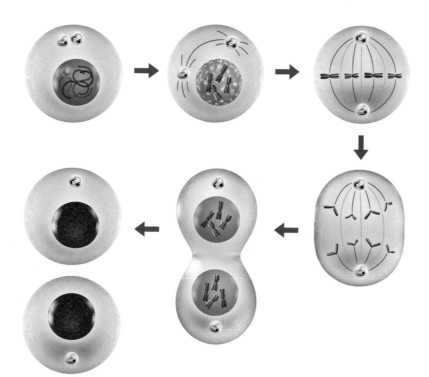

SIDEBAR: DID YOU KNOW?

- An adult human being has more than 37 trillion cells.
- In addition to biology, the scientist Robert Hooke did important in many other fields, including astronomy, geometry, and physics.

TISSUES

Tissues are a group of similar type of cells that perform similar functions. Tissues that are similar combine and form organs. Tissues cover the surface of the body and its organs, and they line the internal spaces. They provide insulation to the body, store fat and energy, and help in motion and posture. There are four types of tissues in the human body: epithelium, connective, muscle, and nervous tissue.

Epithelial Tissues

Epithelial tissues cover the external and internal surfaces of the body and its organs. They are made of cells that are closely packed together and arranged in one or more layers. They do not have blood vessels but can absorb nutrients from other tissues lying underneath.

Functions

Epithelial tissues protect the body from the outside world

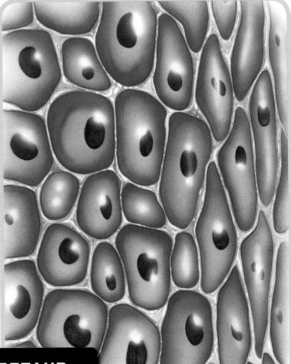

 WORDS TO UNDERSTAND

digestive tract: a long tubelike structure made up of different organs.
glands: parts of the body that produce substances such as hormones.
immunity: the body's ability to resist infection.
musculoskeletal system: the system that comprises the skeleton and muscles of the body.

and can regenerate, such as skin. They absorb nutrients from the **digestive tract**, so that the body can remain in good health. These tissues absorb the remaining nutrients from the kidneys and filter out the waste. They form glands that secrete hormones in the body.

Connective Tissues

These tissues are made of three types of fibers—collagenous, reticular, and elastic. As their name suggests, they connect one part of the body with another. Blood, bones, tendons and ligaments, and cartilage are examples of connective tissues.

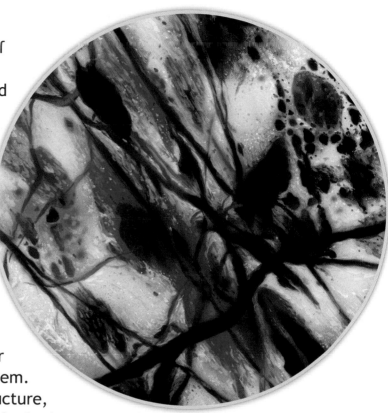

Functions

Connective tissues store nutrients. They also cover the organs and protect them. These tissues provide structure, strength, and support to the body.

Muscle Tissues

Muscle tissues are made of cells that are able to contract and relax to allow movement. They provide flexibility to the body and help in carrying blood and food to the body organs.

Skeletal Muscle Tissue

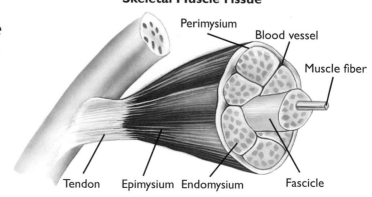

Perimysium
Blood vessel
Muscle fiber
Tendon Epimysium Endomysium Fascicle

Muscle tissues also play a pivotal role in the digestion of food. There are three types of muscle tissues: smooth, skeletal, and cardiac.

Functions

Smooth muscles are involuntary muscles that are found almost all over the body, such as in the stomach, the digestive system, eyes, and blood vessels. Skeletal muscles are voluntary muscles that make up the **musculoskeletal system** of the human body. Cardiac muscles are found only in the heart. They contract to push out blood from the heart, and they relax to allow blood to enter the heart.

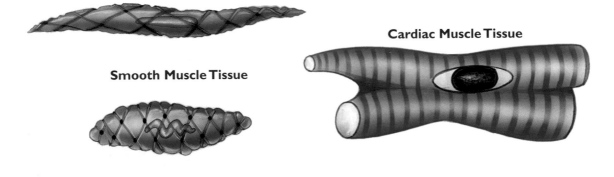

Cardiac Muscle Tissue

Smooth Muscle Tissue

Watch a video about how neurons work.

Nervous Tissues

Nervous tissues are composed of highly mobile cells called neurons and glial cells. Neurons are responsible for carrying messages in the form of electric impulses from the brain and other parts of the body and vice versa.

Functions

Glial cells provide neurons with **immunity** and nutrition. They are also capable of regenerating in the case of an injury.

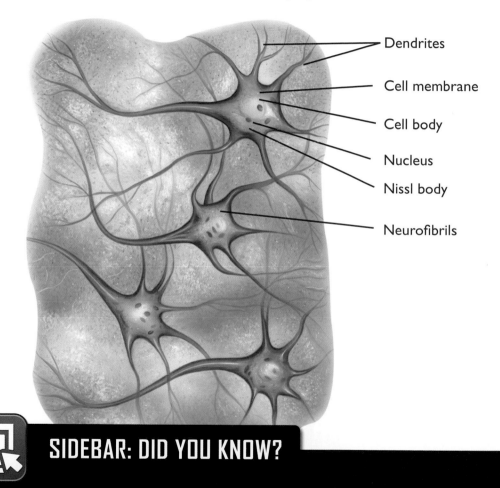

Dendrites

Cell membrane

Cell body

Nucleus

Nissl body

Neurofibrils

BLOOD

Blood is a connective tissue made up of millions of cells. It flows throughout the body in the blood vessels and supplies nutrients and oxygen to cells and tissues. Blood also collects waste products excreted by the cells and filters them out of the body. It constitutes around seven percent of the total body weight. The heart pumps blood at a constant rate and supplies it to the whole body. Blood has four components: red blood cells, white blood cells, platelets, and plasma.

Red Blood Cells

Red blood cells (RBCs) are small, flat, disk-shaped cells, also called erythrocytes. They contain a type of protein called hemoglobin that gives blood its red color. It is responsible for carrying oxygen throughout the body. The level of hemoglobin in the blood also determines its

 WORDS TO UNDERSTAND

antibodies: proteins produced by white blood cells to fight off infections.
hemoglobin: a protein that carries oxygen around the body.
marrow: the substance inside bones, where blood cells are created.
platelets: small, oval-shaped cells.

oxygen-carrying ability. It also helps in transporting carbon dioxide from tissues back to the lungs. RBCs do not reproduce. They have a lifespan of 120 days.

White Blood Cells

White blood cells (WBCs) are responsible for fighting off germs and infections. They can move in and out of the bloodstream to reach the infected part of the body. There are several types of WBCs, which perform different functions. Their lifespan varies from a few days to months. WBCs such as granulocytes and lymphocytes fight harmful microorganisms as well as destroy infected cells. Lymphocytes produce special proteins called **antibodies**, which recognize any foreign invaders (such as viruses) and destroy them. These cells remember the invaders and prepare the body in case the same invaders attack again. WBCs are also called leukocytes.

Production of Blood

Blood cells are produced in the **marrow** of many large bones. Bone marrow is a soft substance inside the bones that produces about 95 percent of blood cells. The first stage of blood cells are called stem cells. As they grow, they develop into RBCs, WBCs, and **platelets**. The process of making new blood cells is called hematopoiesis.

Platelets and Plasma

Platelets help in the process of blood clotting. They are also called thrombocytes. These cells survive for only nine days and are constantly being replaced by new cells. If a blood vessel breaks, platelets come together to stop the bleeding both inside and on the surface of the body. Plasma, on the other hand, is a yellow-colored fluid that contains nutrients, proteins, hormones, and waste materials.

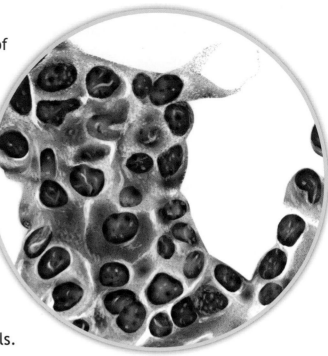

Blood Types

Blood types are determined by the presence of an antigen in red blood cells. Antigen is a substance that is capable of stimulating an immune response. Different people have different types of RBCs and antigens in them. The four major types of blood types are A, B, AB, and O.

SIDEBAR: DID YOU KNOW?

- A newborn baby has around half a pint (250 ml) of blood, whereas a grown-up has about ten pints of blood (five liters) in the body.
- People who have type AB blood are universal recipients, meaning their bodies can accept transfusions from people of any blood type. People with O blood type are universal donors, meaning anyone else can accept transfusions with their blood.

BONES

Bones are hard, **endoskeletal** connective tissues. They are made of calcium, phosphorus, sodium, some other minerals as well as a protein called collagen. They make up the skeletal system that holds the whole body together. Muscles, tendons, **ligaments**, and cartilage join the bones in a skeleton. Muscles are made of long, thin cells called muscle fibers. Ligaments connect bones, and tendons connect muscles to bones.

Types of Bone Cells

Bones are continually growing and reshaping as an individual grows. The three types of cells found in bones are osteoblasts, osteocytes, and osteoclasts. Osteoblasts are responsible for making new bones and help in repairing damage. Osteocytes, on the other hand, carry nutrients and waste materials to and from the blood vessels in the bone. Bone cells that are responsible for breaking down bone through the process of bone resorption are called osteoclasts.

Bone Cell

WORDS TO UNDERSTAND

endoskeletal: relating to the inner skeleton of the body consisting of bones and muscles.

facilitate: to help something else to happen.

ligaments: a type of tough but flexible connective tissue.

Bone Tissues

There are three types of bone tissues with different densities: compact, spongy, and subchondral tissues. Compact tissue is dense, hard, and forms the protective exterior of bones. Spongy tissues are found inside the compact bones and are very porous. The third type of bone tissue is subchondral, which is a smooth tissue and is covered with another type of tissue called cartilage.

Structure of Bones

- **Epiphysis**—the 'head' of the bone.
- **Cancellous bone**—the spongy bone where blood cells are made.
- **Epiphyseal plate**—the area where bones grow in length.
- **Diaphysis**—the bone shaft.
- Compact bone—gives strength to the hollow part of the bone.
- **Periosteum**—the protective layer where ligaments and tendons attach themselves to the bone.
- **Marrow cavity**—contains the yellow bone marrow where white blood cells are made.

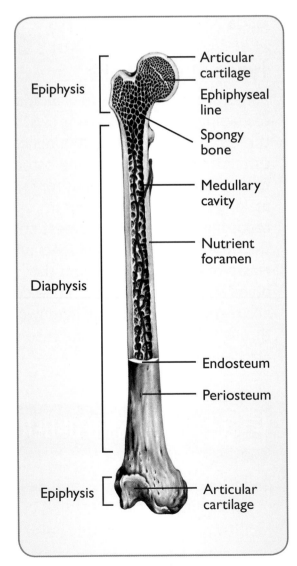

Functions of Bones

Bones provide framework to the body. They allow movement while protecting internal organs from injury. They are the storehouse of calcium and phosphorous, and the production center of red blood cells. Red blood cells are produced in the marrow of many bones, such as thighbones.

Joints in the Body

The place where two bones meet in the body is called a joint. Joints hold bones together and **facilitate** movement. There are three types of joints.

Movable joints: These joints can move freely in different directions. The hip, shoulder, elbows, wrist, knees, and ankles contain free-moving joints. They are also called synovial joints as they are filled with synovial fluid, which helps them move freely.

Partially movable joints: These joints cannot move much and are joined by cartilage. The joints in the spinal cord are an example of such joints.

Immovable joints: These joints do not move at all. For example, the skull is made of many bones which are fixed together and do not move in order to protect the brain. Such joints are linked with a fibrous connective tissue that holds the bones together.

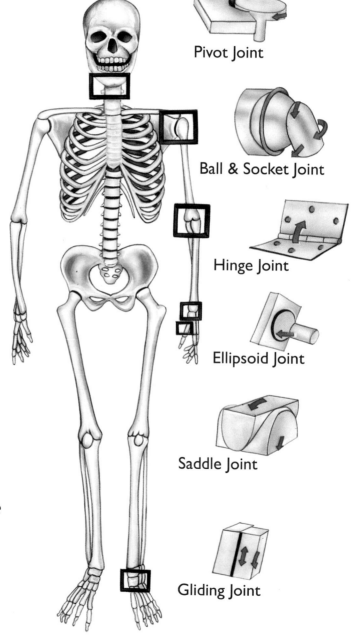

Pivot Joint

Ball & Socket Joint

Hinge Joint

Ellipsoid Joint

Saddle Joint

Gliding Joint

Healthy Bones

Foods rich in calcium, such as dairy products, should be eaten to maintain bones. Exercising is one of the easiest ways to keep bones strong. Physical activity keeps the body active and energetic. Wearing protective gear while playing sports or exercising will help to prevent bone injury. Drinking plenty of water and juices helps in keeping the bones healthy.

This video will teach you about the skeletal system.

TENDONS, LIGAMENTS, & CARTILAGE

Ligaments, tendons, and cartilage are connective tissues composed of soft collagenous tissues. Ligaments connect bones to other bones, and tendons connect muscles to bones. Cartilage, on the other hand, cover bones at the joints. All three of them play a key role in body movements and are a significant part of the musculoskeletal system.

Tendon

Millions of collagen fibers arranged in a parallel form make up tendons. They are strong, flexible tissues and can withstand extreme stress and tension. They grow into the bone and form a tough and permanent mineralized connection, which is difficult to break. Tendons connect bones to muscles. When muscles contract, tendons pull on bones, which causes the parts of the body to move.

WORDS TO UNDERSTAND

hyaline: describes things that have a glassy appearance.
intervertebral: located between vertebrae.
trachea: a tube that brings air to the lungs; also called the windpipe.

Ligament

Ligaments have bundles of collagen fibers, but unlike in tendons, the fibers are arranged in a criss-cross manner in ligaments. They are elastic and flexible to allow freedom of movement, but are not too strong and are unable to extend. Even though their primary function is to keep the joints together, they hardly play a role in the movement of movable joints unless the muscles are breached. When under stress, ligaments lengthen, but they return to their original shape when stress is removed. However, when stretched beyond a certain point for too long they tend to lose their original shape. Thus, dislocated joints should be treated as soon as possible, or else the joints will weaken and become more prone to injury.

Cartilage

Cartilages are flexible tissues made up of collagen, protein, and sugars. They cover the end of the bones at joints. They also give shape and support to other parts of the body, such as ears, the nose, the windpipe and **intervertebral** discs. Cartilages help bones to glide over each other for a smooth movement. They also prevent bones from rubbing against each other. There are three types of cartilage: **hyaline**, elastic, and fibrocartilage.

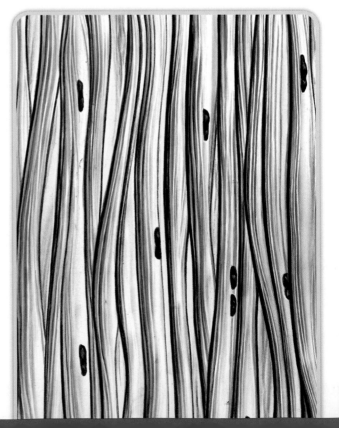

Types of Cartilage

Hyaline cartilage is found in joints and inside bones. It is responsible for the growth of bones, reduces friction at joints, and allows bone movement. Cartilaginous rings on the **trachea** and bronchi help to keep the tubes open.

Elastic cartilage is found in the outer ear, larynx, and epiglottis. It maintains the shape of the organs and provides them with strength and support.

Fibrocartilage is found in the sites connecting tendons or ligaments to bones. It absorbs shock, provides strength and movement, and deepens sockets to avoid dislocation.

Fascias

Fascias are thin, fibrous, connective tissues that surround and support muscles, blood vessels, and nerves. They enable muscles to move smoothly and help in transmitting movements from muscles to bones. Fascias also protect nerves and blood vessels as they pass through and between muscles.

SIDEBAR: DID YOU KNOW?

- The Achilles tendon, which connects the calf muscle to the heel bone, is the longest tendon in the body.
- Andreas Vesalius published a book on human anatomy, *De humani corporis fabrica*, in 1543. In the book, he explained tendons as well as the rest of human anatomy in detail.

BRAIN

The human brain is one of the most complex and important organs of the human body. It is the center of the nervous system encased in the **cranium.** The brain controls all the actions of the body and helps one to learn, think, speak, and recall. The body sends messages to the brain with

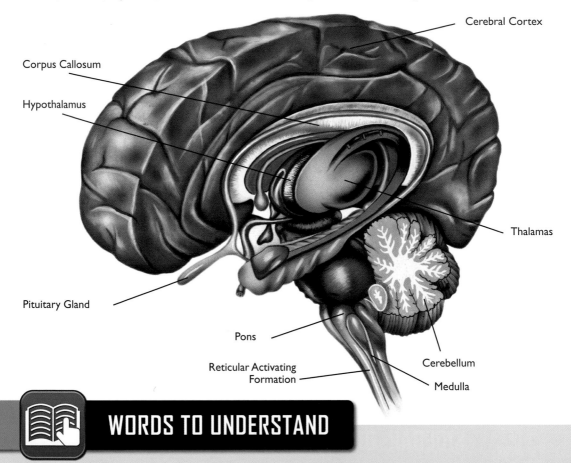

Cerebral Cortex

Corpus Callosum

Hypothalamus

Thalamas

Pituitary Gland

Pons

Cerebellum

Reticular Activating Formation

Medulla

WORDS TO UNDERSTAND

balanced diet: a diet that has all the nutrients and minerals required by the body.

cranium: the skull, especially the part covering the brain.

inquisitive: interested or highly excited to know about something.

metabolism: all the physical and chemical processes that occur to maintain life.

the help of nerve fibers. The human brain has millions of nerve cells that interpret and process these messages and guide the body accordingly.

Structure of the Brain

The brain stem is located at the base of the brain and regulates the body's involuntary actions, such as breathing and heartbeat.

The cerebellum is the second largest part of the brain. It is responsible for maintaining balance and coordinating muscle movement.

The cerebrum is the largest part of the brain. It is responsible for thinking, speaking, storing memory, sensing information and movement. It is divided into four parts, which are known as lobes.

Lobes of the Brain

The brain is divided into four lobes.

The frontal lobe is located in the front part of the brain. It performs many complex functions such as reasoning, problem-solving, feelings, movement, expression of language, parts of speech, and so on.

Parietal lobe

Frontal lobe

Occipital lobe

Temporal lobe

The occipital lobe is located at the back of the brain and is responsible for interpreting visual stimuli and information. This lobe is responsible for interpreting visual images.

The parietal lobe is located in the upper middle part of the brain. It processes sensory information such as pressure, touch, and pain.

The temporal lobe is located on the two sides of the brain and is responsible for interpreting sounds and language, perception, and the formation of memories.

Functions of the Brain

The brain acts as a storehouse of memory. Both short-term and long-term memories are stored in the cerebrum. This organ enables people to ask question by making them curious and **inquisitive**. It controls the balance, movement, and coordination of muscles. The system of regulating body temperature and **metabolism** is also controlled by the brain. It is responsible for performing body functions that are required to stay alive, such as breathing, digesting food, and circulating blood.

The Brain: Left and Right Sides

The left side of the brain controls the right side of the body, whereas the right side of the brain controls the left side of the body. Most people are right-handed because the left side of brain usually predominates the right half. However, in some people, it is the other way around; this explains why certain people are left-handed.

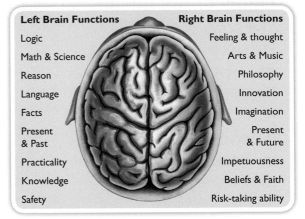

Left Brain Functions	Right Brain Functions
Logic	Feeling & thought
Math & Science	Arts & Music
Reason	Philosophy
Language	Innovation
Facts	Imagination
Present & Past	Present & Future
Practicality	Impetuousness
Knowledge	Beliefs & Faith
Safety	Risk-taking ability

A Healthy Brain

Eating a **balanced diet** and sleeping well are important. Regular exercise increases blood circulation and keeps the body agile. Exercising helps to reduce stress levels and make people happy by the release of hormones called endorphins. Solving puzzles, crosswords, playing scrabble, and reading books or magazines keep the brain healthy.

SIDEBAR: DID YOU KNOW?

- **The brain of a human adult weighs as much as three pounds (1.3 kilograms).**

  People who can easily write with both their hands are called ambidextrous.

HEART

The human heart is one of the most vital organs in the human body. Placed in the center of the chest behind the breastbone and between the lungs, it lies in **pericardial cavity** surrounded by the **ribcage**. The heart pumps and purifies blood, which is then carried all over the body by the blood vessels. The heart, blood, and blood vessels make up the circulatory system of the body.

Structure of the Heart

Chambers: There are four chambers in the human heart. They are filled with blood. The upper chamber is called the atrium, which is divided into left and right atria. The lower chamber is called the ventricle, which is divided into left and right ventricles.

Blood vessels: Some large blood vessels are connected to the heart transport blood throughout the body. The two main arteries are the aorta and the pulmonary artery. The aorta transports oxygenated blood to the rest of the body, while the pulmonary artery carries blood to the lungs to extract oxygen. On the other hand, the blood vessels that bring blood back to the heart are called the "vena cava," meaning they are the veins of the heart.

Valves: These connect the atria to the ventricles. The mitral valve separates the left atrium from the left ventricle, while the tricuspid valve separates the right atrium from the right ventricle. The aortic

 WORDS TO UNDERSTAND

abdominal: relating to the part of the body, that contains the major organs of the body like stomach, liver, kidney, pancreas, etc.
pericardial cavity: the cavity or empty space present around the heart.
ribcage: bones that curve around the chest to protect organs such as heart and lungs.

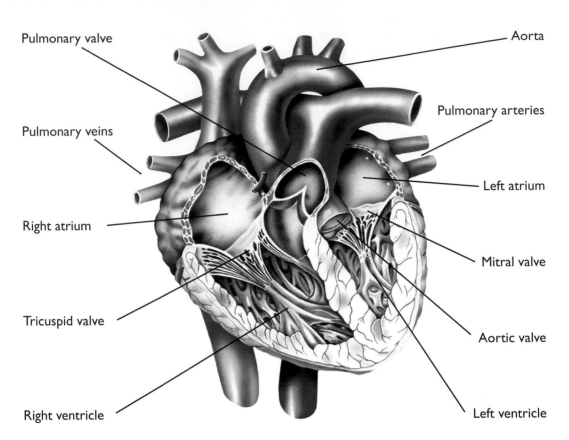

Pulmonary valve

Aorta

Pulmonary arteries

Pulmonary veins

Left atrium

Right atrium

Mitral valve

Tricuspid valve

Aortic valve

Right ventricle

Left ventricle

valve and pulmonary valve, on the other hand, are in charge of controlling the flow of blood as it leaves the heart.

Heart wall: A thick wall of muscles separates the left and right sides of the heart. It is also called the septum.

The Cardiac Cycle

The sequence in which the heart is filled with blood, which is then pumped out with the help of blood vessels, is called the cardiac cycle. It has two phases: the diastole phase and the systole phase. In the diastole phase, the ventricles relax and fill with blood from the atria. In the systole phase, the ventricles contract and send the blood out of the heart. The mitral and tricuspid valves close to block the entry of blood back into the atria. When the ventricles finish contracting, the aortic and pulmonary valves close to block blood from going back into the ventricles. What we call the heartbeat is made by the contraction of the ventricles and valves.

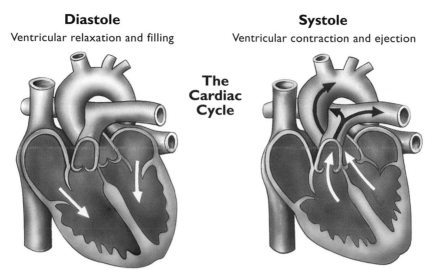

Diastole
Ventricular relaxation and filling

The Cardiac Cycle

Systole
Ventricular contraction and ejection

Pacemaker

A pacemaker is a small device used by people with abnormal heart rate. It uses electrical impulses to help the heart to beat at a normal pace. It is usually placed inside the chest or the **abdominal** area. A pacemaker consists of a battery, generator, and wires. The generator sends electrical impulses that set the heartbeats. The wires carry impulses back and forth from the heart to the generator.

A Healthy Heart

Healthy foods such as avocados, oranges, and broccoli help to keep the heart healthy. Doing plenty of exercise and playing sports helps in overall fitness. It is advisable to avoid smoking and drinking alcohol. Fatty foods, such as burgers and french fries, should also be avoided.

 SIDEBAR: DID YOU KNOW?

- The heart beats continuously about 100,000 times a day and 35 million times a year.
- Blue whales have the largest hearts of any animal. A blue whale's heart is around the size of a compact car.

LUNGS

Lungs are one of the main respiratory organs in the human body. They absorb oxygen from air and transport it throughout the body through blood vessels. Lungs also extract **deoxygenated** air from blood and remove it from the body. On average, humans inhale and exhale oxygen about 22,000 times a day, expelling around 300 cubic feet (8.5 cubic meters) of air.

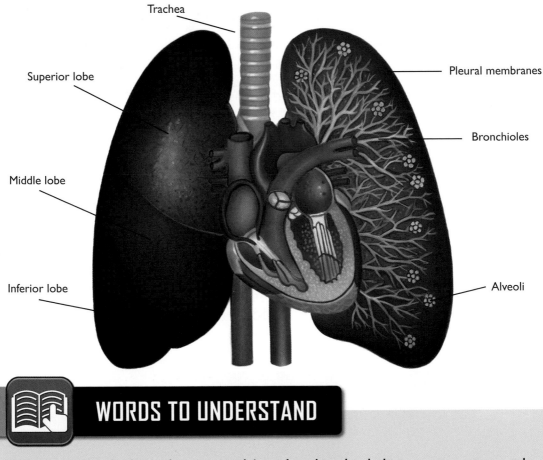

Trachea

Superior lobe

Middle lobe

Inferior lobe

Pleural membranes

Bronchioles

Alveoli

WORDS TO UNDERSTAND

deoxygenated: describes something that has had the oxygen removed from it.

diaphragm: a muscle just above the stomach.

respiration: breathing.

Structure of the Lungs

The lungs are divided into lobes. The right lung has three lobes—superior, middle, and inferior lobes, whereas the left lung has two lobes—superior and middle lobes.

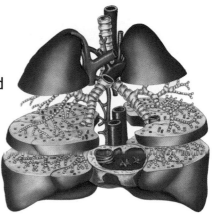

The trachea is also known as the windpipe. The air reaches the lungs through the trachea.

The bronchi are tubes that branch off from the trachea and carry oxygen deeper into the lungs.

The bronchioles are tiny tubes branching off from the bronchi. They carry oxygen more deeply into the lungs.

The alveoli are clusters of air sacs that lie at the end of each bronchiole. They transfer oxygen and absorb carbon dioxide from the blood.

The pleural membranes cover the lungs and let them slide around easily during the inhalation and exhalation of air.

How Does One Breathe?

When a person inhales, the **diaphragm** contracts and pulls the rib cage up and down. The space within the chest increases which reduces the air pressure inside the lungs. Air goes through all the bronchi and bronchioles and fills up the millions of alveoli. When a person exhales, the diaphragm relaxes and the rib cage moves up and down. The space within the chest decreases, which increases the air pressure inside the lungs.

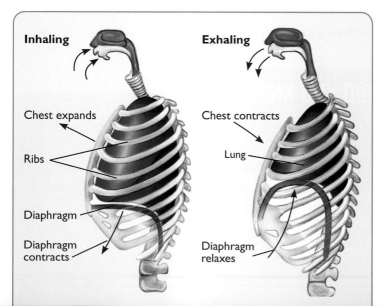

Inhaling

Exhaling

Chest expands

Chest contracts

Ribs

Lung

Diaphragm

Diaphragm contracts

Diaphragm relaxes

Functions of the Lungs

The main function of the lungs is **respiration**. The air we breathe contains several gases, including oxygen. Lungs add fresh oxygen to the blood, which then carries it to the cells. Lungs also exhale carbon dioxide from the body. They help in speaking as air from the lungs is pushed up the throat and through the vocal chords that produce sound. They also secrete immunoglobulin, which protects the body against respiratory diseases.

Diaphragm

The diaphragm is a rounded muscle that lies between the lungs and the abdomen. It helps the lungs to inhale and exhale. The diaphragm contracts when a person inhales air and expands when the air is breathed out. When we hiccup, the diaphragm and the nearby muscles quiver, causing us to breathe air suddenly. It hits the vocal cords and produces a 'hic' sound.

Healthy Lungs

To keep the lungs healthy and free from diseases, it is advisable to avoid smoking and places where other people are smoking. Always wear face protection when working with chemicals.

 SIDEBAR: DID YOU KNOW?

- In 1243, Arabic physician Ibn al-Nafis was the first to describe the process of taking in oxygen and removing carbon dioxide from the body, otherwise known as pulmonary circulation.
- The study of lung diseases is known as pulmonology.

KIDNEYS

The kidneys are one of the most crucial organs of the human body. They are bean-shaped organs found at the end of the ribcage, close to the vertebral column on each side of the abdominal cavity. The average kidney is roughly 4 inches long (around 10 to 11 centimeters), and is similar to the size of a computer mouse. Kidneys are necessary for the proper functioning of the **urinary system**.

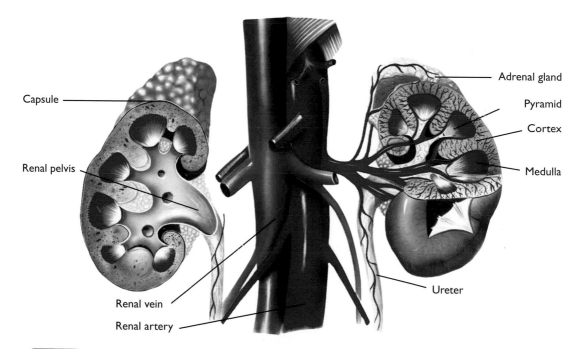

Capsule

Adrenal gland

Pyramid

Cortex

Renal pelvis

Medulla

Renal vein

Renal artery

Ureter

 WORDS TO UNDERSTAND

capillaries: very small blood vessels.

dialysis: a process of cleaning wastes from the blood artificially, when the kidneys are not functioning.

urinary system: a body system that removes unwanted, undigested, waste; includes organs such as the kidneys and the large intestine.

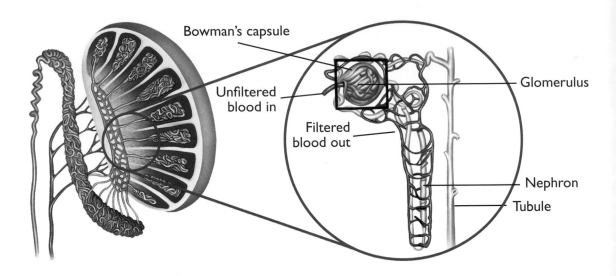

Bowman's capsule

Unfiltered
blood in

Filtered
blood out

Glomerulus

Nephron

Tubule

Structure of the Kidneys

Renal capsule—the thin membrane covering the kidneys.

Medulla—the inner region of the kidneys, which is red and brown in color.

Renal pelvis—a funnel-shaped cavity that collects the urine drained from kidneys.

Nephrons—the basic structural and functional units of the kidney.
Bowman's capsule—it lies inside the nephrons and contains glomerulus.

Glomerulus—a network of **capillaries**. The glomerulus filters and cleans blood as it flows through the kidneys.

Nephrons

Nephrons are long, tubelike structures. Each kidney contains about one million nephrons. They eliminate wastes from the body, and regulate blood pressure and the pH level of the blood. A nephron filters around 180 liters of blood a day. All the blood in the body is filtered more than 20 times a day. Transporters are specialized proteins found in different parts of a nephron. They reabsorb all the minerals and nutrients from the filtered blood.

Kidney Dialysis

When kidneys do not function properly due to a damage or failure, **dialysis** is required. Dialysis machines act as artificial kidneys. Hemodialysis and peritoneal dialysis are the two main types of dialysis. Both the types of dialysis filter blood and remove harmful wastes, extra salt, and water. In hemodialysis, a machine is used, while in peritoneal dialysis, the abdomen lining called peritoneal membrane is used.

Functions of Kidneys

Filtering blood and controlling blood pressure by regulating the salt content in the body is one of the primary functions of the kidneys. They also produce hormones such as erythropoietin, which signals the bone marrow to make red blood cells, renin, which helps regulate blood pressure, and an active form of vitamin D that helps control the level of calcium in the body. They maintain homeostasis in the body, which means that they balance the water content in the body by filtering out water and removing waste. They regulate the composition of blood as well as concentrations of various ions and other important substances.

Healthy Kidneys

It is important to drink plenty of fluids to keep kidneys in good health. Healthy foods rich in vitamins and minerals are good for kidneys, as is regular exercise.

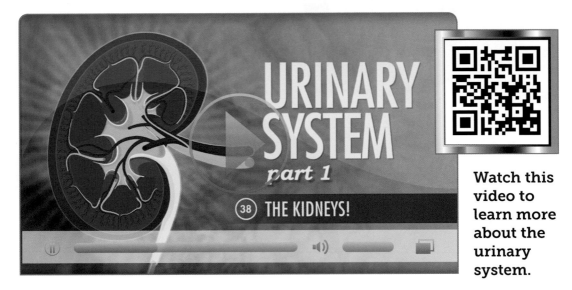

URINARY SYSTEM
part 1

(38) THE KIDNEYS!

Watch this video to learn more about the urinary system.

SIDEBAR: DID YOU KNOW?

- The most common causes of kidney disease are diabetes and high blood pressure.
- Renal physiology is the study of kidney functions.

STOMACH

The stomach is a like a balloon filled with air that holds the food while it is digested. It is a part of the digestive system and lies between the **esophagus** and the small intestine. The stomach does not have a fixed shape; the shape changes according to the posture of the body and the quantity of food inside it.

Parts of the Stomach

The stomach has two parts: stomach walls and gastric folds. Stomach walls are lined with three layers of muscles. The walls contract and expand along with the layer of muscles. These movements help in breaking down the food into smaller particles. Gastric folds are the largest part of the stomach and help in grinding and digesting food with the help of gastric juices.

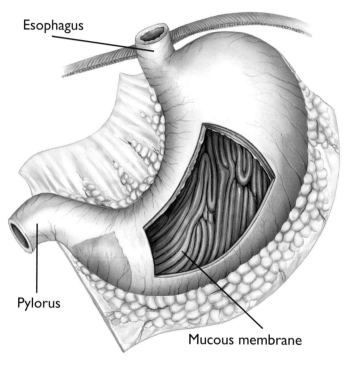

Esophagus

Pylorus

Mucous membrane

WORDS TO UNDERSTAND

esophagus: a long canal that connects the mouth to the stomach.

enzymes: substances produced by the body to create particular effects, such as digestion.

mucus: a slimy substance created by the body for lubrication.

Gastric Juices

Different cells in the stomach make different gastric juices such as **enzymes**, acids, and **mucus** to break down food. Pepsin is an enzyme that breaks down proteins contained in food. It works with the help of an acid called hydrochloric acid. The stomach linings produce this acid. To protect itself against the damage caused by acids, the stomach produces mucus. It serves as a cooling agent that protects the inner linings of the stomach.

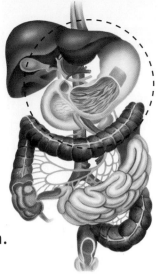

How Does the Stomach Work?

Food enters the stomach through the esophagus. The stomach mixes the food with water and gastric juices and begins to break down food into proteins. It also releases hydrochloric acid that kills harmful bacteria and other harmful microbes. It protects itself from being digested by its own enzymes and acids by releasing mucus. The layer of mucus lines the inner walls of the stomach and neutralizes the acids. The stomach produces a thick creamy fluid called chyme. It, then, slowly releases chyme into the small intestine. It is also helps the small intestine absorb nutrients.

Layers of the Stomach

The stomach is composed of layers. The innermost layer is called the mucosa layer where stomach acid and digestive juices are produced. The next layer is submucosa layer, which is surrounded by muscularis. Muscularis is the layer of muscle that mixes food in the stomach. Subserosa and serosa are tissue layers that form the wrapping of the stomach. Serosa is the outermost layer of the stomach.

Functions of the Stomach

The primary function of the stomach is churning food and releasing nutrients into the body. Our stomach churns the food and releases it in the form of chyme. Chyme contains water, hydrochloric acid, and some digestive enzymes. It triggers the production of bile to break

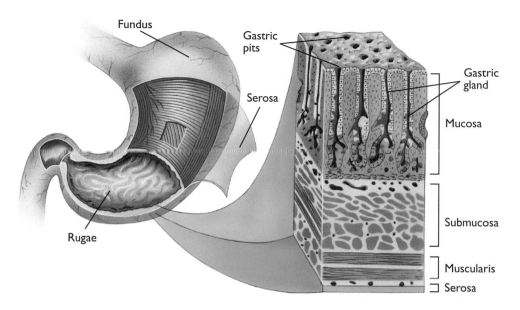

Fundus

Gastric pits

Gastric gland

Serosa

Mucosa

Rugae

Submucosa

Muscularis

Serosa

down the remaining food matter. The hydrochloric acid produced by the stomach linings helps in killing germs that can cause illness. The stomach linings also produce mucus, which in turn prevents the acidic gastric juice from leaking out of the stomach, and harming the organs. The stomach linings produce mucous membranes every two weeks.

A Healthy Stomach

A balanced diet rich in nutrients and fiber content, such as fresh fruits, vegetables, and whole grains keeps the stomach healthy. Chewing food properly before swallowing also helps in smoothing and speeding up the process of digestion. Consumption of milk, yogurt, and other fluids keeps the stomach healthy. People should avoid eating foods rich in fats, such as fries or burgers, on a regular basis.

SIDEBAR: DID YOU KNOW?

- Gastritis is an inflammation of the stomach caused by irritation in the stomach lining.
- The stomach can hold about a quart (about one liter) of food at a time.

LIVER

The liver is one of the largest internal organs of the human body. It is composed of millions of blood vessels, capillaries, and cells. A healthy liver weighs about 3 pounds (around 1.3 kilos) and is reddish-brown in color. It filters over a liter of blood every minute, secretes many useful fluids, stores energy in the form of glucose, and performs many others necessary functions in the body.

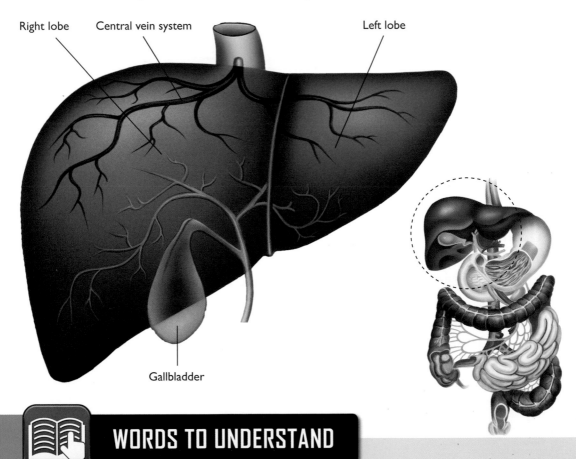

Right lobe   Central vein system   Left lobe

Gallbladder

WORDS TO UNDERSTAND

cholesterol: a waxy, fat substance found in all tissues.
gallbladder: a small organ beneath the liver.
pancreas: a large gland that secretes digestive fluids.

Role in Food Digestion

The liver plays an important role in the digestion of food, along with the **pancreas** and the **gallbladder**. It processes nutrients absorbed into the blood and uses carbohydrates to produce glycogen. Glycogen is a form of energy which is released when required by the body. The liver also secretes a digestive fluid called bile—a dark-green or yellow liquid that breaks down fats in food.

Pancreas

The pancreas is an organ of the digestive system, and the Islets of Langerhans are a group of cells in the pancreas that produce the hormone called insulin. Insulin facilitates the digestion of food and also regulates the level of sugar in blood.

Gallbladder

The gallbladder is a small pear-shaped muscular sac located just under the liver. It is an organ of the digestive system. A digestive juice called bile is stored in the gallbladder.

Functions of the Liver

The liver performs hundreds of functions without taking a break. It cleans blood, destroys worn-out red blood cells, and aids the production of new red blood cells and clotting factors. It breaks down nutrients to be used by other body parts as well as produces antibodies to fight off infections. It also breaks down fats into fatty acids and produces **cholesterol**.

This multifunctional organ produces vitamin B$_{12}$, which is important for the production of red blood cells. It filters unwanted chemicals such as alcohol and removes it from the body as waste.

A Healthy Liver

Overeating can negatively affect the health of the liver, as can consuming alcohol in large amounts. A high-protein diet that includes eggs, cereals, legumes, and grains can help keep the liver healthy. Drinking plenty of fluids and exercising helps in maintaining a healthy weight.

SIDEBAR: DID YOU KNOW?

- The liver is the only organ in the human body that can regenerate itself.
- When you take medication, it is broken down in the liver.

EYE

Human eyes are the second most complex organ of the body after the brain. Eyes detect light and help us to see the world around us. They use the light coming from an object to determine its shape, size, color, and brightness. They have a spherical shape and each eye weighs about a quarter of an ounce (about seven grams).

Parts of the Eye

The sclera covers most of the eyeball.

The cornea is the transparent covering of the eye that helps it to focus.

The iris is a muscle that surrounds the pupil and controls the amount of light entering the eye.

The pupil lets the light enter the eye.

The lens is the transparent **biconvex** body that focuses the rays of light on the back of the eyeball.

The retina contains million of light-sensitive cells and is at the back of the eye.

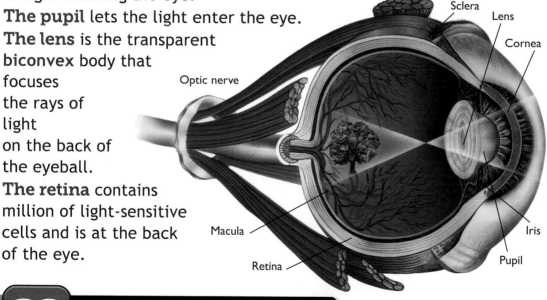

Sclera

Lens

Cornea

Optic nerve

Macula

Retina

Iris

Pupil

How Do We See?

Light rays enter the eye through the cornea, which bends them into a narrower beam. Now the light rays travel through the pupil, which allows them to enter the eye. It grows smaller or larger with the help of the iris. The pupil **dilates** in dim light, to allow more light to enter the eye. The light rays strike the lens, which bends the light rays into an even narrower beam. Then the light rays reach the retina which contains cells called rods and cones. These cells are extremely sensitive to light and absorb the light rays, forming an upside-down image. The image is then sent to the brain via nerve impulses along the **optic nerve**. The brain interprets the messages and converts them into the things we see.

Where Do Tears Come From?

Tears are the secretions of the eye that clean and moisten the eye, which is necessary for clear vision. They are produced in the lacrimal glands, which lie at the corner of the eyes. Tears are then carried to the surface of the eyes by lacrimal ducts, which run between the eyes and nose. When eyes are welled up with tears, the lacrimal ducts drain out the excess. Sometimes when we cry a lot, the lacrimal ducts are not able to drain out all the tears. Thus, they end up coming out from the nose, leading to a "runny nose."

Why Do We Cry?

If dust or some other particle is stuck in the eye, tears are generated to get rid of the foreign material. Irritation and dryness in the eyes can also be caused by smoke, cold winds, the common cold, and allergies. Onions make people cry because when cut they release a **volatile** chemical compound, which reacts with the water in the eyes.

Eye Care

Eating foods rich in iron, as well as vitamins A, E, and C, is a great way to improve vision. People should protect their eyes from dust, pollution. Wearing protective eyewear while swimming, skiing, or playing any other sport that could damage the eyes is also important.

SIDEBAR: DID YOU KNOW?

- The retina has about 120 million rods and between 6 and 7 million cones.

- Cones are the receptors that enable you to perceive color. People who are "color blind" lack sensitivity in their cones.

EAR

Ears collect sounds, process them, and send them as signals to the brain. Ears are also helpful in maintaining the balance of the body. Earwax is produced in the ear canal; it protects the parts of the ear from dust, insects, and infections.

Parts of Ear

External ear—pinna, external auditory canal.
Middle ear—tympanic membrane (eardrum), **ossicles**, eustachian tube.
Internal ear—cochlea, semicircular canals.

How Do We Hear?

Sound waves are collected by pinna and are directed to the external auditory canal. Inside the auditory canal, the sound waves are amplified and hit the tympanic membrane, or eardrum. The eardrum then passes the vibrations through ossicles into the internal ear. The internal ear is also called the labyrinth and contains thousands of tiny hair cells. The hair cells convert vibrations into nerve impulses, which are transferred along the auditory nerve to the brain. The brain recognizes these nerve impulses as sounds and also helps us distinguish between different types of sound.

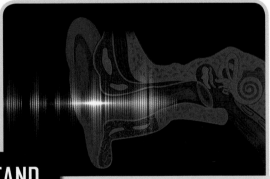

 WORDS TO UNDERSTAND

cochlea: the part of the ear that turns sounds into nerve impulses.
ossicles: three small bones inside the ear.
pinna: the part of the ear on the outside of your head; also called the auricle.

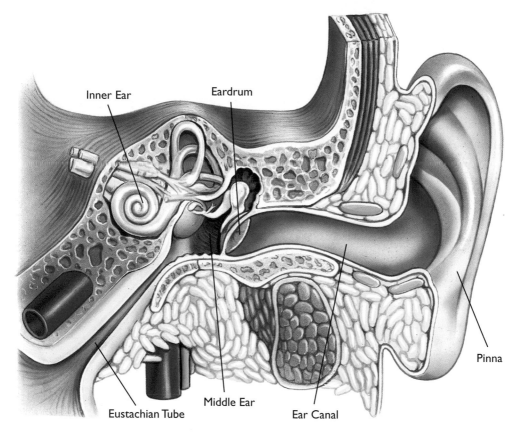

Inner Ear

Eardrum

Pinna

Eustachian Tube

Middle Ear

Ear Canal

Balancing Organs

The ears are also known as the balancing organs of the body. The inner part of the ear helps in maintaining physical balance. The internal ear is made up of several loops and small canals. Three small canals are present above the cochlea and are known as semicircular canals or the vestibular labyrinth. The semicircular canals contain a clear liquid and several tiny sensory hair cells. The liquid flows in different directions when we move our head. This liquid moves the sensory hair cells, which send a message to the brain about the movement and position of our head through the vestibulocochlear nerve. In a microsecond, the brain sends messages to the muscles so that we keep our balance.

The Balancing System

The balancing system of the body is dependent on three principal organs of the body: eyes, muscles and joints, and the inner ear. The eyes tell us what we are looking at, muscles and joints tell us about our body posture, and the inner ear tells us about our position and other ongoing movements. The eyes work together with the vestibular labyrinth to keep objects from blurring when we move our heads. The balancing system also keeps us alert about our position when we are walking or taking an amusement ride. The brain receives all the messages, then interprets and processes them to maintain balance.

Caring for Ears

• People should wear earplugs in noisy places, such as during loud music concerts or around noisy machinery. Listening to loud music using earphones or headphones should also be avoided.

• It is advisable to avoid poking ears with pointed objects. Poor use of earbuds or cotton swabs to clean ears can damage them.

• People with partial or full hearing disability should wear hearing aids.

This video explains how sound works and how we can hear it.

 SIDEBAR: DID YOU KNOW?

• Our ears get larger as we age.
• The most common cause of hearing loss is exposure to loud noises.

NOSE

The nose helps in the **inhalation** and **exhalation** of air, and it warms and cleans the air you breathe in. This is how the lungs are protected from air that is dry or cold. The nose also enables a human being to smell as many as one trillion types of smells.

Parts of the Nose

Nostrils: The two holes or openings of the nose are known as nostrils. The air that we breathe enters our nose through the nostrils.

Nasal passage: The nostrils lead the air through the nasal passage, which is lined with several hairs called cilia that prevent harmful substances from entering the body.

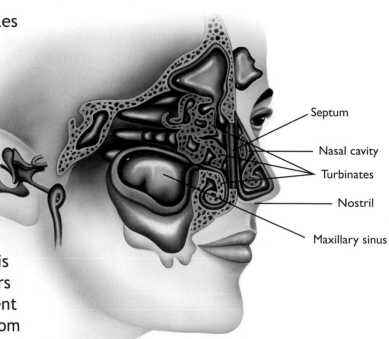

Septum

Nasal cavity

Turbinates

Nostril

Maxillary sinus

 WORDS TO UNDERSTAND

exhalation: the act of releasing breath.
inhalation: the act of taking breath in.
olfactory: relating to the sense of smell.

Nasal cavity: The nasal cavity is an empty space in the nose that is filled with air and is separated from the mouth through the presence of a hard palate in the mouth.

Mucous membrane: The mucous membrane is a thin, moist, and sticky layer of tissue that lines the inner nose. It captures dust, germs, and other small particles and prevents them from reaching the lungs.

Septum: The septum is the thin cartilaginous tissue the separates the nasal cavity in the nostrils.

Soft palate: The soft palate is the soft region present behind the tongue that closes the nasal cavity when food is swallowed.

Hard palate: The hard palate is the hard bony structure that separates the oral cavity and the nasal cavity.

How Do We Smell?

The odor of various substances present in the air enters the nose and reaches the nasal cavity. Inside the nasal cavity, the odor meets the **olfactory** epithelium, which sits at the roof of the cavity. The olfactory epithelium contains millions of tiny sense receptors that detect smell. They are of different shapes and possess the ability to detect particular smells. The odor receptors detect smell, convert it into electric signals, and sends signals to the olfactory bulb through the olfactory nerves. Then the olfactory bulb sends these signals to the other parts of brain, which recognizes these signals and tells us the nature of the smell.

Sense of Smell

Our sense of smell makes us aware of the aromas of different food items, fruits, vegetables, as well as flowers and scents. The sense of smell also protects us from inhaling foul smells and harmful gases. In certain professions, a keen sense of smell is essential, such as firefighting, florists, and perfumers.

Caring for the Nose

Wear face masks while traveling in polluted areas. Face masks also prevent people from sniffing allergens such as pollens and dust. When suffering from cold, use a nasal spray but avoid overusing it. In addition, don't blow the nose very hard or put small objects inside the nose as it might damage the nose or cause infections.

Types of Smells

Although there are at least a trillion different smells in the world, most of them can be categorized into one of the following types.

- Fragrant
- Fruity
- Citrus

- Woody
- Chemical
- Sweet

- Minty
- Toasted/nutty
- Pungent
- Decayed

SIDEBAR: DID YOU KNOW?

- Cats have twice as many smell receptors as humans do.
- Nosebleeds occur when a blood vessel breaks in the septum region. It can occur due to colds, dry air, certain allergies, and even excessive exercise.

TONGUE

The tongue is the sensory organ for taste. It is rough in texture but appears smooth due to the presence of a mucous membrane that keeps the tongue moist. Our tongue is made up of the strongest muscles of the body. The upper part of the tongue is covered with **papillae**, which contain taste buds. They help us enjoy different types of foods.

Functions of the Tongue

Our tongue helps us chew food by mixing it with saliva, crushing it against the roof of the mouth, and pushing it towards the teeth for grinding. It also detects when the food is ready for swallowing and then pushes the chewed food towards the food pipe. In addition, the tongue plays a vital role in helping us to speak. The muscles of the tongue change shape to produce different sounds. The tongue can also sense touch, temperature, and pressure. It is also responsible for fighting infections with the help of lingual and palatine tonsils. They filter germs and fight off infections.

Taste and Smell

When a person chews food, odor chemicals are released that trigger the sense of smell through a channel that connects the nose to the top of the throat. If this passage is blocked by a cold or flu, odor chemicals cannot reach the olfactory sense detectors.

WORDS TO UNDERSTAND

innumerable: too many to count.
microscopic: describes something so small it is not visible by the naked eye and can be seen only through a microscope.
papillae: small, fleshy bumps.
ulcer: a type of sore.

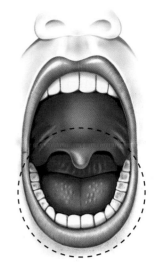

Large
Taste
Buds

Small
Taste
Buds

Sense of Taste

Our tongue is covered with **innumerable** taste buds. These are a clusters of cells that are connected to the brain through nerves. As a result, the tongue is able to distinguish four types of tastes: sweet, bitter, salty, and sour. Umami is a fifth type of taste that is experienced by eating a chemical called glutamate, which is present in meat extracts and chicken broth.

The sense of taste and smell together attracts us to foods that smell delicious as well as warns us not to eat rotten or spoiled food. Eating cold food alters our taste perception for a few minutes.

How Do We Taste?

Taste buds are present inside the papillae on the tongue. They are also present on the hard upper surface of the mouth, inside the cheeks and along the lining of the throat. Each taste bud is a collection of several taste cells, also known as gustatory cells, that are capable of detecting a particular taste. Each taste cell has highly sensitive **microscopic** hairs called microvilli. These hairs become active when they meet the food chemicals as the food mixes with the saliva. Then each taste cell responds to a particular taste and sends nerve impulses to the brain. The brain receives the nerve impulses and interprets the taste of the food we are eating.

Healthy Tongue

Cleaning the tongue with a tongue cleaner or toothbrush removes the bacteria build-up, leftover food, and dead cells from the tongue. It is as important as cleaning teeth and is the most effective way of getting rid of bad breath. People should also avoid eating very hot, cold, or spicy food items as it may damage taste buds, which can cause loss of the sense of taste. In addition, one should avoid sharing food with people who are suffering from mouth **ulcers** or any other mouth infections.

SIDEBAR: DID YOU KNOW?

- There are about 10,000 taste buds inside the mouth, which replace themselves every two weeks.
- Frenulum is a thin fold of the membrane that is present on the lower side of the tongue, and attaches the tongue to the floor of the mouth.

SKIN

Human skin is the largest and most flexible organ of the body. It acts as a wall between our body and the outside world. Skin covers and protects the internal organs of the body from germs, extreme temperatures, and other harmful agents. Hairs, nails, sweat glands, and oil glands are also parts of the skin. The skin on the palms of the hand and the soles of the feet is the thickest, while the skin of the eyelids is the thinnest in the body.

Layers of Skin

There are three types of skin: epidermis, dermis, and the subcutaneous tissue. The epidermis is the outer layer of the skin. It is made up of millions of cells that are constantly dying and being replaced. The epidermis contains three main types of cells: melanocytes, keratinocytes, and Langerhans.

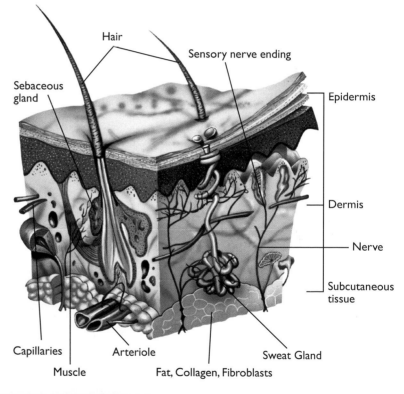

Hair
Sensory nerve ending
Sebaceous gland
Epidermis
Dermis
Nerve
Subcutaneous tissue
Capillaries
Muscle
Arteriole
Fat, Collagen, Fibroblasts
Sweat Gland

WORDS TO UNDERSTAND

exposure: contact with something.
hygiene: cleanliness.
pigment: a substance that gives color to something, such as skin.

The dermis is the layer that lies beneath the epidermis. It is made up of blood vessels, capillaries, lymph nodes, oil glands, sweat glands, and connective tissues. The layer of skin below the dermis is the subcutaneous tissue. It is the innermost layer of the skin and is made up of cells that store fat. It is responsible for regulating the body temperature and connects the skin to all the other tissues present beneath it.

Sense of Touch

The sense of touch is derived through the presence of skin on our body. The skin has millions of nerve endings that aid in sensory reception. These nerve receptors carry messages to the brain, which guide us about the type, texture, and temperature of the object we are touching.

Skin Color

The skin contains a color **pigment** called melanin, which is responsible for the color of the skin. The amount of melanin determines the fairness or the darkness of the skin. The more the melanin, the darker the skin. The skin is fairer when it has less melanin. Its amount can also be increased temporarily by sun **exposure**; this results in the production of more melanin, thereby causing a suntan.

Creases and Fingerprints

Creases are a type of skin patterns, such as frowning or smile lines, that develop where the skin is folded over a long period of time. They are also present on the palms, soles, knees, forehead, and elbows. However, fingerprints are crisscross patterns on the tips of fingers. They are formed when the baby feels pressure on his developing fingers inside the womb. The fingerprints do not change and can never be altered because their pattern is set in the skin's dermis. No two people in the world have exactly the same fingerprints.

Skin Care

Good hygiene is one of the easiest ways of keeping skin healthy and germ-free. Taking baths regularly, scrubbing the skin as well as washing hair keeps the skin and hair clean. People should wear sunscreen when going out in the sun to prevent suntan or sunburns.

SIDEBAR: DID YOU KNOW?

- The integumentary system is the protective system of the body. It comprises the skin, hair, nails, and sweat glands.
- Wrinkles are the permanent folds of the skin that appear during old age.

INTESTINES

The intestines are part of the digestive system and help in the digestion of food as well as the removal of waste from the body. They are divided into the small intestine and the large intestine. The small intestine is a long, muscular tube located between the stomach and the large intestine. The large intestine collects waste and processes it into feces.

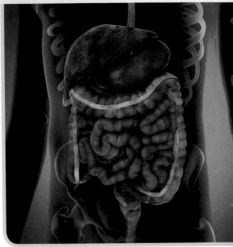

Parts of the Small Intestine

The duodenum is the first part of the small intestine.

The jejunum is the coiled middle part of the small intestine. It is also the largest part.

The ileum is the last part of the small intestine and is located in the lower abdomen. The ileum has a length of about 11 feet (3.5 meters).

Function of the Small Intestine

The small intestine is responsible for absorbing most of the nutrients in our food. The digested food from the stomach empties into the duodenum. Duodenum receives the pancreatic enzymes from the pancreatic duct and bile from the liver and the gallbladder. The inner linings of the jejunum andthe ileum are covered with small, fingerlike

 WORDS TO UNDERSTAND

bicarbonate: a type of salt.

hormone: a chemical substance in the body that causes some type of physical reaction.

villi: small, fingerlike projections on the lining of the small intestine.

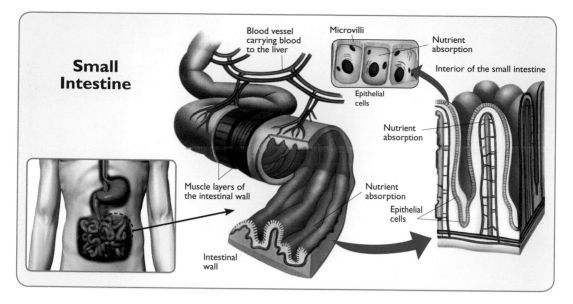

Small Intestine

Blood vessel carrying blood to the liver

Microvilli

Nutrient absorption

Interior of the small intestine

Epithelial cells

Nutrient absorption

Nutrient absorption

Muscle layers of the intestinal wall

Nutrient absorption

Epithelial cells

Intestinal wall

projections called **villi**. When the food is broken down into nutrient components such as vitamins, minerals, salts, and waters, the villi absorb these nutrients. Food such as fiber, that is not digested, goes to the large intestine.

Parts of the Large Intestine

The caecum is located in the right lower abdomen. It receives waste material from the small intestine.

The colon is located in the abdominal cavity. It moves the waste material from the small intestine to the rectum.

The ascending colon is located at the bottom of the abdomen, to the right, and ascends towards the liver.

The transverse colon extends across the abdomen, from right to left.

The descending colon goes downwards, to the left of the abdomen.

The sigmoid colon is located at the bottom of the abdomen, to the left.

The rectum is located below the abdomen, where feces is stored before being passed as a bowel movement.

Functions of the Large Intestine

The large intestine works to absorb water from digested food and to maintain the balance of fluids in the body. It absorbs certain

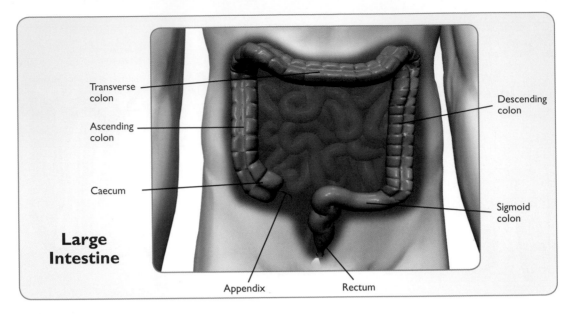

Transverse colon

Ascending colon

Caecum

Large Intestine

Descending colon

Sigmoid colon

Appendix

Rectum

vitamins, including Vitamin B^{12}, Vitamin K, thiamin, and riboflavin. Waste matter is stored in the large intestines until it is discharged from the body.

Bacteria in the Large Intestine

The large intestine contains a large number of beneficial bacteria, such as enterobacteria, streptococcus faecalis, bacteroides, bifidobacterium, and eubacterium. These bacteria provide the enzymes for digesting many molecules and utilizing nutrients. Beneficial bacteria also prevent the growth of harmful bacteria and intestinal inflammation.

SIDEBAR: DID YOU KNOW?

- Despite its name, the small intestine is the longest section of the digestive tract.
- Secretin is a digestive hormone produced by the small intestine in response to the acid from the stomach.
  It triggers the pancreas to release fluid and bicarbonate, which neutralize the acid.

NEURONS

Neurons are those nerve cells that carry **electrochemical** signals throughout the nervous system. They are the building blocks of the brain. There are around a hundred billion neurons in the brain. Their capability to pass electrochemical signals through longer distances makes them different from other cells.

Neurons: Parts & Functions

Nucleus: contains the genetic material used to create proteins for the cell.

Cell body (also called soma): contains the nucleus, RNA, DNA, and organelles. All the information gathered by dendrites is collected here. The cell body decides whether to send the received signals.

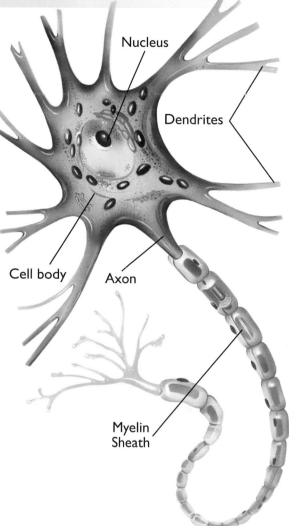

Nucleus

Dendrites

Cell body

Axon

Myelin Sheath

WORDS TO UNDERSTAND

electrochemical: relating to chemical changes that are caused by electricity.

peripheral: outlying.

vesicle: a cavity or sac that is filled with fluid or air.

synapse: a tiny gap between nerve cells.

Dendrites are spikes or branches projecting from the cell body like the branches of a tree. Most cell bodies have about six dendrites. These dendrites are responsible for making connections with other cells; these connections allow neurons to communicate with each other. They are also called nerve endings and can be present on one or both ends of a cell. A single neuron can have connections with as many as 2,000 other neurons at the same time.

Axons are long, wirelike projections that carry electrochemical messages or nerve impulses away from the cell body. Depending on the type of neuron, axons vary greatly in length. Some are very short, whereas some can stretch from the base of the brain to the tip of the toes. When a neuron sends a signal, it is the job of the axon to carry it to all the neurons connected with that neuron.

The myelin sheath is a thin layer of fat that cover portions of axons. It provides strength to axons and helps them in carrying nerve impulses with great speed. However, not all neurons have myelin sheaths.

Neurotransmitters

Neurotransmitters are chemicals that transmit signals from one neuron to another. They are produced inside the cell body and are transferred through axons. When the neurotransmitters reach axon endings, they are stored in bubbles called **vesicles**. There are empty spaces between neurons, which are called **synapses**. Neurotransmitters cross over the synapses to reach another neuron.

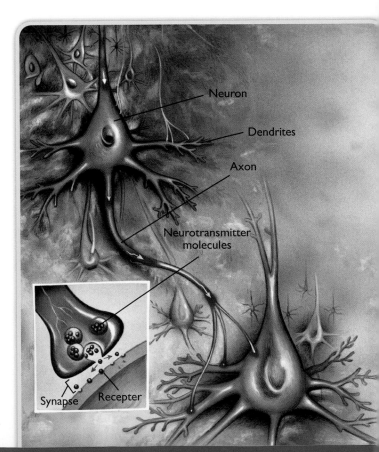

Neuron

Dendrites

Axon

Neurotransmitter molecules

Synapse   Recepter

Types of Neurons

Sensory neurons: These neurons transmit information from the skin, muscles, joints, and so on to the central nervous system. They indicate pressure, pain, and temperature. There are sensory neurons present in the eyes, nose, and ears, which enable one to see, smell, and hear.

Motor neurons: These neurons transmit information from the central nervous system to the **peripheral** organs, such as muscles, intestines, and organs, such as the heart. They control muscle contractions.

Interneurons: These neurons pass information from sensory neurons to motor neurons. They also carry information to other interneurons. Most interneurons are found in the central nervous system and connect neurons of the brain and the spinal cord.

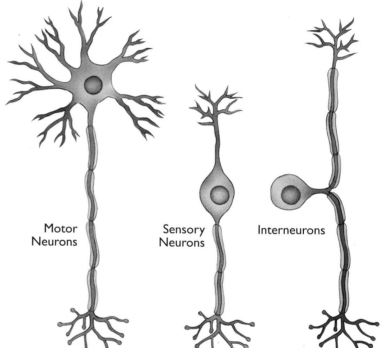

Motor Neurons   Sensory Neurons   Interneurons

SIDEBAR: DID YOU KNOW?

- Neuroglia is a type of cell in the nervous system that provides a support system for neurons.
- Neurogenesis is a process of growing new neurons throughout life.

SPINAL CORD

The spinal cord is a long, thin bundle of nervous tissue that extends from the base of the brain to the lower back. This large bundle of nerves is protected by the vertebral column, which is also called the backbone or spinal column. Three layers of **meninges** cover the spinal cord as well as the brain. The brain and the spinal cord together make up the central nervous system.

Dimension

The spinal cord is about the diameter of a human finger and is shorter than the spinal column. On an average, the spinal cord is about 17 inches (45 centimeters) long.

Vertebral Column

The spinal cord resides in the vertebral column, which is made up of separate bones known as vertebrae. At birth, we have 33 separate vertebrae, but some of them fuse together over time. The vertebral column is divided into four regions—**cervical**, **thoracic**, lumbar or lower back, and sacral (pelvic). A clear fluid called cerebral spinal fluid surrounds the spinal cord and acts as a cushion to protect it against damage from the vertebrae.

 WORDS TO UNDERSTAND

cervical: relating to the neck.
conduit: a passageway.
meninges: the system of membranes that covers the central nervous system.
thoracic: relating to the thorax, or chest.

Functions of the Spinal Cord

The spinal cord performs three functions. First, it acts as a medium to send and receive information provided by motor neurons, which travel down the spinal cord. Second, it acts as a **conduit** to send and receive sensory information provided by sensory neurons, which travel upward, toward the brain. Third, the spinal cord acts as a center for coordinating reflexes.

Spinal Nerves

Spinal nerves, or nerve roots, carry the information from the spinal cord to the rest of the body, and from the body back to the brain. There are 31 pairs of spinal nerves containing sensory and motor nerve fibers that connect the spinal cord to the rest of the body. Spinal nerves branch off from different regions of the vertebral column and cater to the different parts of the body.

- **Cervical region**—the back of the head, neck, shoulders, arms, hand, and diaphragm.
- **Thoracic region**—the chest and the abdomen.
- **Lumbar region**—the lower back and parts of thighs and legs.
- **Acral region**—the pelvis and most parts of legs and feet.

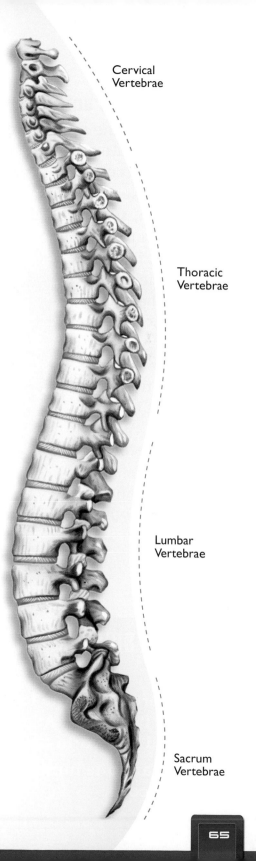

Cervical Vertebrae

Thoracic Vertebrae

Lumbar Vertebrae

Sacrum Vertebrae

Ascending and Descending Tracts

The nerves of the spinal cord are grouped into ascending and descending tracts. Ascending tracts provide sensory information, such as touch, pain, temperature, and so on, from the body to the brain. On the other hand, descending tracts carry information from the brain to the rest of the body. They are responsible for regulating movements and controlling body functions.

SIDEBAR: DID YOU KNOW?

- The vertebra at the top of the spinal column supports the head. It is called Atlas, in reference to the Greek god who carried the world on his shoulders.

- There are one hundred billion neurons in the human spinal cord.

DONATION & TRANSPLANTATION

Organ **transplantation** is a process in which a damaged or failing organ is surgically removed and replaced with a new organ. This procedure has saved the lives of hundreds of thousands of people around the world. Organ transplantation is indeed one of the greatest advances in the field of medicine.

What is a Graft?

Grafting is the process of removing tissues from a part of the body and implanting them to replace the damaged tissue on another part of the body. The process of grafting is similar to a transplant. However, grafting is different from organ transplantation because it involves removal and replacement of only a portion of an organ, and not the whole organ.

 WORDS TO UNDERSTAND

immunosuppressant: describes something that interferes with the functioning of the immune system.

rejection: here, when the body refuses to accept a transplanted organ.

transplantation: the act of taking living tissue from one organism and putting it in another.

Types of Transplant

Kidneys are the most commonly transplanted organs, but many others are transplanted also, including the lungs, heart, liver, pancreas, intestine, cornea, skin, bone, thymus, bone marrow, blood, and heart valves. There are two main types of transplants: autografts and allografts. Autografts are transplants in which organs or tissues are transplanted within the same person's body. Transplants between two different human beings are called allografts.

Organ Donation

Organ donation is a voluntary action that can improve as well as save multiple lives. Healthy organs or tissues can save someone who is in critical need of them. Most organ and tissue donations can happen only after the donor has died. Organ donation can be of two types: living organ donation and posthumou,s or cadaveric, organ donation.

Living Organ Donation

Living organ donations are made by a donor who is alive. Most people who choose to become living organ donors are often related to the patient. Parents, spouses and close friends, or relatives express their will to donate their organs out of love and care for the patient. However, some people have even donated their organs to strangers. There are two ways living donors can donate their organs. One, they can donate organs that come in pairs, such as kidneys. Second, the donor can donate a part of an organ that will still be able to function, for example, a lobe of lungs or liver.

Cadaveric Organ Donation

In Latin, the word *cadaver* means "dead body." A person who decides to donate his organs and tissues after death is called a cadaveric organ donor. The organs that are taken from deceased people are called cadaveric organs. In some countries, even if a person has not indicated a preference for organ donation, after his death the family members can decide whether his organs can be donated or not.

Why Donate Organs?

Organ donation can save as well as improve the lives of many ailing people. It is the noblest help human beings can offer to each other. Today, millions of people, including children, are waiting for organ transplants, but there are not enough organ donors to help them. Organ donation and transplantation provides a new lease on life to people. However, not many people are aware of the process of organ donation and its importance. The need for organs is much greater than their availability. This calls for increased awareness of the importance of organ donation. Small efforts in this direction can help in saving countless lives.

Transplant Rejection

Transplant **rejection** can occur when the body's immune system begins to attack the newly transplanted organ or tissue. The body's defense system fights the transplanted organ and tries to get rid of it if

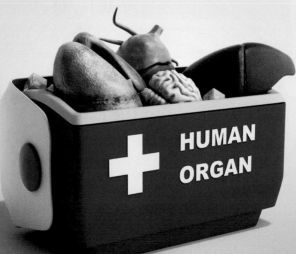

it has a harmful bacteria or virus. It makes antibodies to attack and kill the transplanted organ, which may prove to be fatal. Therefore, in order to protect the new organ from antibodies, doctors prescribe **immunosuppressant** medicines. These medicines reduce the number of antibodies and suppress the immune system so that the transplanted organ can work properly.

Life after Transplant

People who have received an organ or tissue transplant can go on to live a normal and healthy life. They can work, play, and travel like any other healthy person. However, they will have to take extra care for a certain period after the transplant and may have to take lifelong medication to prevent organ rejection.

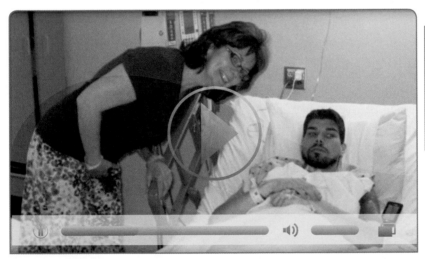

This video will tell you more about living donor transplants.

SIDEBAR: DID YOU KNOW?

- There are more than 30,000 transplants in the United States every year.
- Cornea transplants are usually not rejected by the immune system since corneas do not have blood supply.

ARTIFICIAL LIMBS

A prosthetic or artificial device is designed to replace a missing body part or to make a part of the body work better. The term 'prosthesis' involves the replacement of any body part, such as eyes, ears, nose, fingers and toes. Artificial limbs are replaced most commonly.

Who Needs Prosthetics?

Unfortunate events such as accidents and wars are two common reasons why people lose their limbs or damage their other body parts. Soldiers fighting wars are very often met with accidents. In towns, road accidents are one of the main causes of **amputation**. However, in some cases, amputation is due to a **congenital defect**. Anybody who wants to recover a lost body part can use prosthetics.

 WORDS TO UNDERSTAND

amputation: the practice of surgically removing a limb due to a severe injury or illness.
congenital defect: a medical condition that someone suffers from since birth.
PVC (polyvinyl chloride): a type of plastic.
silicon: a nonmetallic element.

Importance of Prosthesis

Prosthesis has been one of the most advanced discoveries in medical history. It gives a new life to physically challenged people. It encourages these people to lead normal lives. People with prosthetic limbs can walk, run, drive, climb stairs, and swim. They can go to school and do many other activities like their peers.

Cosmetic Prosthetics

Cosmetic prosthetics are artificial limbs that look real. These limbs are made of **silicon** or **PVC (polyvinyl chloride)** and are designed to resemble real hands or legs with matching skin tone, veins, hair, fingerprints, and even moles and freckles. Customized cosmetic prosthetics look more realistic than the standard ones but are also more expensive.

Robotic Prosthetics

Current research is focused on the next generation of robotic prosthetics, which will be controlled by thought, just like real limbs.

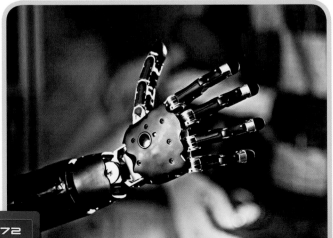

With robotic prosthetics, a person can control his movements through muscular contractions, which trigger nerve impulses from the brain and help in movement—similar to what happens in natural body movements.

Physical Therapy and Care

To live a normal life with a newly acquired artificial limb, one has to learn to use it properly and take care of it. There are special exercises to strengthen the muscles to move the artificial limb for performing everyday activities. People with artificial legs must learn to walk, get into and out of bed, climb stairsand get up safely if they fall.

SIDEBAR: DID YOU KNOW?

- The oldest known prosthetic was made in Egypt more than 3,000 years ago.
- Below-the-knee amputation is the most common type.

TEXT-DEPENDENT QUESTIONS

1. What is cell theory?

2. What are the four types of tissues?

3. What are the different functions between red blood cells and white blood cells?

4. What can you do to keep your bones healthy?

5. What is cartilage?

6. What are the parts of the brain?

7. What role do bronchi and bronchioles play in breathing?

8. Why are some people color blind?

9. How do we taste food?

10. What is the cochlea?

RESEARCH PROJECTS

1. Find a diagram of the human body online and print it out.
Using this text and other sources, label the organs described in this
book. Use the contents page so you don't forget any.

2. Find out more about the life and work of one of the scientists
mentioned in this text, such as Robert Hooke, Andreas Vesalius,
or Ibn al-Nafis. Write a short report about one of them. How did his
discovery come about? How did his work change the world?

3. Using the tips in this book and other sources, find out about
things people can do to keep their organs healthier.   Make a list of
those tips and then turn it into a poster to educate people on how
to keep themselves and others healthier.

4. Pick an organ or system described in this
book and find out more about it. How does it
work? What can go wrong with it and what
can be done to fix any problems?

5. Research the history of organ
transplantation. Find out when the
first transplants of major organs
occurred (for example, kidney, liver,
lung, heart, and so on). Turn your
research into a timeline.

FURTHER READING

Human Body! New York and London: DK Children, 2017.

Kenney, Karen. *The Circulatory System*. Minneapolis, MN: Jump!, Inc, 2017.

Mooney, Carla. *The Brain: Journey Through the Universe Inside Your Head*. White River Junction, VT: Nomad Press, 2015.

Weird But True Human Body. National Geographic Kids: Washington, DC, 2017.

INTERNET RESOURCES

BBC Science: Human Body & Mind
http://www.bbc.co.uk/science/humanbody/
A thorough site about human anatomy, including online games where you can test your knowledge of organs and body systems.

Teen Health and Wellness
http://www.teenhealthandwellness.com/
A comprehensive site with tons of information about the body and health.

TeensHealth: Body Basics
http://kidshealth.org/en/teens/body-basics.html
A thorough overview of the human body, including key organs and systems.

Picture Credits:

INDEX

A

antibodies, 14–15, 41, 70
   See also immune system

B

bacteria, 38, 60, 70
balance system, 47–48
bile, 41, 58
   See also gallbladder
blood cells, 11
   plasma, 16
   platelets, 16
   production of, 15
   red, 14–15
   white, 15
blood types, 16
bones, 17–20
   See also endoskeletal system
botanist, 6
brain, 24
   functions of, 26
   health of, 26
   structures of, 25

C

capillaries, 33
cardiovascular system
   See also heart
cartilage, 17, 21–23
cells
   characteristics, 7
   life cycle, 9
   structures of, 6, 8
   theory, 7
   types of, 7
cholesterol, 40–41
color blindness, 45

D

dialysis, 33
diaphragm, 30, 32
diet, 24, 26, 39, 42
digestion, 41, 58–60
digestive tract, 10–11, 36–39, 52
   See also intestines
donation. See transplanting

E

ears, 46–48
   balance system of, 47–48
   health of, 48
   hearing, 46
   parts of, 46–47
electrochemical signals, 61–62
endoskeletal system
   bone structure, 18
   bone tissues, 18
   bones, 11
   health of, 19
   joints, 19
   marrow, 15
   types of cells, 17–18
enzymes, 37–38
esophagus, 37
exercise, 26, 29, 36, 51, 73
eyes, 43–45
   health of, 45
   parts of, 43
   tears, 44
   vision, 44

F

fingerprints, 57

G

gallbladder, 40–41, 58
glands, 10, 55
grafting, 67

H

hair, 55
healthy habits
   for brain, 26
   for heart, 29
   for kidneys, 36
   for liver, 42
   for lungs, 32
   for nose, 51
   for skin, 57
   for stomach, 39
   for tongue, 54
hearing, 46

heart
   cycles of, 28–29
   health of, 29
   pacemaker, 29
   structures of, 27–28
Hooke, Robert, 7
hormones, 41, 60

I
Ibn al-Nafis, 32
immune system, 10, 13, 15, 32, 68–70
immunoglobulin, 32
integumentary system, 57
intestines, 58–60
   large
      functions of, 59–60
      parts of, 59
   small
      functions of, 58
      parts of, 58

J
joints, 19

K
kidneys, 33–36
   dialysis, 35
   functions of, 35
   health of, 36
   structures of, 34

L
Leeuwenhoek, Antonie Van, 7
ligaments, 11, 17, 21–22
liver, 40–42, 58
   functions of, 41
   health of, 42
lungs, 30–32
   function of, 32
   health of, 32
   immunoglobulin, 32
   respiration, 31 *fig*
   structures of, 31

M
marrow, 15
meninges, 64
mucus, 37–38
musculoskeletal system, 10–12

N
nails, 55
neurons, 61–63
   neurotransmitters, 62
   parts of, 61–62
   types of, 63
neurotransmitters, 62
nose, 49–51
   health of, 51
   parts of, 50
   smell, 49–50

O
organ donation, 68–70
organelles, 6, 9

P
pacemaker, 29
pancreas, 40–41, 58
physiologist, 6–7
plasma, 16
platelets, 15–16
prosthetics, 71–73
protozoa, 7

Q
QR Video
   how neurons work, 12
   how sound works, 48
   living donor transplants, 70
   skeletal system, 20
   urinary system, 36

R
respiration, 31 *fig*, 32, 49

INDEX

S

Schleiden, Matthias Jakob, 7
Schwann, Theodor, 7
skeletal system. *See* endoskeletal system
skin, 55–57
    care of, 57
    color, 56
    creases, 57
    touch, 56
    See also integumentary system
smell, 49–52
spinal cord, 64–66
    functions of, 65
    nerves of, 65–66
    parts of, 64
stem cells, 15
stomach, 36–39
    function of, 38–39
    gastric juices, 38
    health of, 39
    parts of, 37
    See also digestive tract

T

taste, 52–54
tears, 44–45
tendons, 11, 17, 21
tissue cells
    connective, 11
        blood, 14
        bones, 17
        cartilage, 21–23
        ligaments, 21
        tendons, 21
    epithelial, 10–11
    muscle, 11–12
    nervous, 13
tongue, 52–54
    functions of, 52
    health of, 54
transplanting, 65–70
    grafting, 67
    types of, 68

U

urinary system, 33, 36

V

vertebral column, 64–65
vision, 44
vocal cords, 32

THE MIRRORSTONE

written by
MICHAEL PALIN

illustrated by
ALAN LEE

conceived & designed by
RICHARD SEYMOUR

ALFRED A. KNOPF · NEW YORK

For Anne

THIS IS A BORZOI BOOK PUBLISHED BY ALFRED A. KNOPF, INC.

Copyright © 1986 by Richard Seymour, Michael Palin, and Alan Lee
All rights reserved under International and Pan-American
Copyright Conventions.
Published in the United States by Alfred A. Knopf, Inc., New York.
Distributed by Random House, Inc., New York.
Published in Great Britain by Jonathan Cape Ltd., London.
Holograms by Light Fantastic Ltd., London.
Manufactured in Great Britain
2   4   6   8   10   9   7   5   3   1

Library of Congress Cataloging-in-Publication Data

Palin, Michael. The Mirrorstone.
Summary: An English schoolboy is snatched into another world by
the magician scientist Salaman, who forces him to brave
underwater terrors in a quest for the priceless Mirrorstone.
[1. Fantasy]   I. Lee, Alan, ill.   II. Title.
PZ7.Pl768Mi   1986   [Fic]   86-7375
ISBN 0-394-88353-5

he first time he saw it was at the swimming pool. He dried his hair as usual, pulled out his Mickey Mouse comb, glanced in the mirror and then started back in shock. For the face he saw looking back at him was not his own. It wasn't very different, but something was wrong. The hair was a bit longer, the cheeks were a bit thinner. "Do I really look as bad as that?" thought Paul, peering closer. And that's when he got an even bigger shock. For as he moved nearer to the mirror the other face stayed still! Paul felt himself go very cold for a moment, then he heard a shout from one of the boys behind him. "Stop staring at yourself, we all know you're ugly!" When Paul looked at the mirror again, there, sure enough, was his own freckly, friendly face.

Paul was the best swimmer in the school. He was especially brilliant at swimming under water. He could swim three lengths of a pool without once coming up for air. In fact that day Paul had spent such a lot of time under water, he wondered if this was why he was seeing things.

he next day something very odd happened again. He was brushing his teeth when he became aware of a strange sensation, as if he were being watched. He looked up and there was the face that wasn't quite his face staring back at him from the mirror. This time it couldn't possibly be him because Paul had a mouthful of water, and the other face didn't. He smiled as best he could, but the face didn't smile back. Suddenly, the bathroom door flew open and his mother rushed in looking for her earrings.

"Are you all right?" she asked. "You look as though you've seen a ghost."

Paul shook his head.

"No…no…I'm fine." he muttered. As soon as his mother had gone he looked back into the mirror. There was nothing there except a schoolboy – with a blob of toothpaste on the end of his chin.

After school that day Paul was walking home past the old T.V. repair shop when he stopped in amazement.

Usually he didn't notice the T.V. repair shop. It was always closed and all the televisions inside were broken anyway, but today something was different. One of the old television sets seemed to be on.

He pressed his nose up against the window. What he saw made him suddenly stiffen. The television wasn't actually on at all.

It was a reflection on the screen.

He could see the cars passing in the road behind him, but where he should have been was the boy from the mirror.

Paul jumped back and for a moment he saw the face reflected on every dusty screen in the shop.

He turned and ran.

He dropped his schoolbag, caught his foot in it, and, falling headlong onto the road, was nearly run over by a 24 bus.

It screeched to a halt and Paul picked himself up and walked on, trembling.

When Paul reached home, instead of throwing his bag at the cat and switching on the television, he threw himself at his mother and clung to her.

"You're old enough to know about crossing the road, Paul, honestly."

Paul held on to her even harder. "I saw something...in the shop..."

"*Seeing* things! Now come on, you're just shaken up and a good thing too. You'll be more careful next time."

Paul decided to tell her everything, about the faces, about the boy he kept seeing. But she was in a hurry as usual.

"I'll be back in half an hour. Be good."

A moment later he heard the door slam.
The apartment was very quiet.
He sat down until he could feel his heart beating more slowly.
His knee hurt. Looking down, he saw a long dark graze.

There was even a smear of blood. He went into the bathroom, switched on the light and pulled open the door of the cupboard where the medicines were kept.

He heard a noise.

At first he thought it was the squeak of the cupboard door. Then it came again.

This time there was no mistaking it. It was a voice yet there was no one else in the house.

It was coming from the direction of the mirror.

Other voices joined in. Paul turned slowly towards the mirror and there was the boy.

"What do you want?" cried Paul.

The boy said nothing but stretched out his hand as if beckoning Paul to follow him.

"Where are you going to take me?" asked Paul, trying to keep his voice from shaking. He followed the boy closer to the mirror, and as he did so an icy breeze blew into the bathroom, although it had no window, and the sound of the voices grew. The bathroom he knew so well began to disappear, the light became brighter, the wind blew stronger and the next moment Paul found himself, blinking, in the middle of a strange city. It was full of towers topped with flags which swirled in the breeze. He recognized nothing and no one. It was like a picture in a history book. He looked behind him, but there was no sign of the bathroom. He looked ahead of him, but there was no sign of the boy.

The voices he had heard belonged to a crowd of people who had gathered and were staring at something in a most unfriendly way. Then he realized that what they were staring at was him. He followed their eyes down to the tips of his white running shoes with the holes in the toes and up past the dirty old jeans to the faded Ghostbusters T-shirt which his mother was always trying to throw away, and he suddenly understood just why they were staring. They'd never seen anyone looking like him before, and they didn't seem to like it.

"Hey, you!" A most evil-looking man stepped forward and came up so close to Paul that he could see bits of cheese in the man's beard. "You're coming with us!"

Paul realized that the only brave thing to do was to run away, and without knowing quite where he was going he raced across the square, through a fountain, scattered a flock of geese, ducked under a balcony and disappeared down a narrow passage. He could hear shouts behind him, getting closer and closer. He caught sight of some stairs leading to a lighted window high up above him and threw himself desperately towards them. The stairs seemed to go on forever, and he was breathing in great gasps as he reached the top and squeezed himself into a darkened doorway. Then the door he was leaning against fell open and he tumbled into a cluttered, cobwebby room, in the middle of which sat a very old man indeed.

"Ah, *there* you are! We've been waiting for you."

he man's hair was long and matted as though it hadn't been washed for years. His face was lined and wrinkled, as if he'd been through a dozen lifetimes, but the eyes that stared at Paul were bright and piercing. Paul was still gazing at him when he felt himself being pulled into the room. His clothes were wrenched off and a thick, itchy brown tunic was thrown over his head. He winced as his arm was twisted behind his back and he was pushed up close to the old man.

"Mary! Don't be so rough with him!" cried the old man.

Turning his head to see who was holding him so tightly, Paul was amazed to find himself looking into the face of a girl, not much older than himself. She looked scornfully down at him as she dropped his faded Ghostbusters T-shirt into the middle of the fire.

The old man nodded at the girl and she released Paul. She reached towards a table full of books and bottles and maps and skulls and picked up a pair of spectacles with very thick lenses which she put on the old man, so that when he looked at Paul his eyes seemed to have grown four or five times bigger. Paul felt that they were staring right through him. The old man looked him up and down. "Yes…yes…you're just the boy we want, Paul…*just* the boy we want."

"How did you know my name?"

"I know everything."

"If you know everything," said Paul, "then where's the boy who brought me here, the boy in the mirror?"

"Oh, you'll find him," said the old man with a thin smile. Paul looked around the room.

It was small and full of measuring instruments, maps, stuffed animals and old timepieces.

Near the window was a telescope of sorts, pointed up into the sky, and beside it a table covered with so many books that it looked to Paul like at least forty-two years' homework.

"You'll find him when you've done what you're here for."

"What am I here for?" asked Paul, trying to sound brave, and failing miserably.

The old man raised his head impressively.

"Let me tell you. My name," he said grandly, "is Salaman." He seemed a bit cross when Paul said "Who?" and Salaman muttered something rude about the way history was taught.

"I am, in my humble way, a genius. I have spent my lives studying glass, reflections…mirrors… the movement of light on surfaces, and I have in my researches discovered the formula for the perfect mirror. A mirror that would show people themselves as they really are. Outside *and* inside." His eyes fixed on Paul. They shone fiercely.

"Have you ever seen yourself as you really are? With all your innermost thoughts and feelings visible? So you can never lie to yourself again?"

Then his eyes clouded over as he went on.

Many years ago, in the city in which I used to live, I made such a mirror. It was small, no bigger than a large pebble. I called it the Mirrorstone. When the king of the city heard of it, he called me to his court and made me his chief magician though I prefer to be called a scientist. But he didn't want *me.* He wanted the Mirrorstone. I knew he would use it only to dominate people, not to increase his understanding of them.

"So I hid the stone from him, and the king swore that if he could not have it, no one should.

"He ordered the city's walls to be destroyed and the Mirrorstone was swept away by the sea. But thanks to Mary's father…"

"*Grand*father," said Mary.

"Yes, of course…I forget how old I am. Thanks to him I escaped with my life, and since then I have been searching for the Mirrorstone every waking hour. And at last I have found it!" With that he lifted a cloth and suddenly the room was full of light. It came from a globe, smaller than a soccer ball.

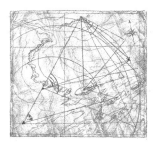

Paul stared open-mouthed.

"Look in here!" cried Salaman in triumph, and drew Paul to his side.

What Paul saw in the globe was an underwater world, as clearly as if he were there himself, and in the center of it all was a jagged black rock at the very edge of which he could see a luminous stone.

"More light!" ordered Salaman. As Mary held a lamp above the globe, the stone began to shine so vividly that it seemed to rise up out of the sea towards them.

"I could touch it!" gasped Paul. "I could hold on to it *now!*"

hy don't you try?" suggested Salaman. Paul reached for the stone and his hands closed around it, but he couldn't hold it. He tried again, but once more it slipped through.

"You will be able to touch it soon," said Salaman and turned his piercing gaze once more on Paul.

"Why do you think I wanted a boy who could swim three lengths without once coming up for air?"

"How did you know I could swim three lengths?"

"I told you, I know everything."

Paul felt a strange chill of fear.

There was something in the old man's smile that was only half friendly.

"And now it's time for you to go," Salaman said.

"Go where?" Paul could feel his heart beating faster.

"Don't worry," said Salaman. "I shall guide you there." But he didn't say anything about coming back.

He beckoned Paul towards the luminous globe. Paul looked at the door, but as he did so, he felt Mary's arm very firmly on his. She held him fast. Then he had a surprise, for instead of leading him to the globe, she pulled him towards her and hissed in his ear.

"Escape…now!" Paul stared back at her.

Mary squeezed his arm again.

"You will never come back alive with the Mirrorstone!"

"I can swim…I can swim three lengths without…"

"It's not the water that is the danger, Paul. There are other dangers, far worse."

"What *other* dangers?" Before she could reply Salaman shouted impatiently from beside the globe.

"Paul!" Mary pushed him towards the door.

Run!" she screamed.

"Mary!" Salaman's voice was full of anger.

And Paul ran.

Ran for dear life, jumping down the stairs to the street, two or three at a time. Running as fast as he could through the narrow streets, while Salaman's voice shrieked high above him.

Paul raced on, looking neither left nor right, fearing that if he so much as caught a glimpse of a window, a glass or a mirror, Salaman might be there. The voice of the old man grew fainter until it disappeared altogether. It was a long time later, as Paul ran down a rain-soaked alleyway, that he first dared look around him, and he never noticed the gleaming puddle until it was too late.

As his foot touched it he felt, with a terrible sense of helplessness, that he was sinking.

o his horror the puddle seemed to be bottomless, and though he kicked and splashed frantically the water rose around him. His hands clawed the sides but he could not save himself and soon he was completely submerged. He felt himself being sucked under and there was nothing he could do but hold his breath as he was pulled down and down.

Then quite suddenly the turbulent water of the whirlpool gave way to a green and clear calm, and there beneath him was the most extraordinary sight. It was a ruined city, more beautiful than anything he'd ever seen.

He swam on down across seaweed-covered towers and broken battlements. Fish glided lazily out of chimneys, and crabs scuttled across disused courtyards. The peacefulness and beauty of it all soothed his fear. What had Mary been so worried about? This was the greatest adventure anyone could have, and he was the luckiest boy in the world!

Paul found himself before the huge doorway of what looked like a royal palace. He swam inside, doing somersaults along the corridors and floating through a room where a throne stood empty, its golden legs encrusted with barnacles. This room led into a tower and Paul swam up the narrow stairs faster and faster, until, spinning round like a top, he burst out into the sunlight above the waves. Then he found himself in a room with a table laden with food and he sat down, thinking, "I must be in Paradise!" But there was something strangely familiar about the room. In one corner was a telescope and by the window were piles of books and papers and bottles and skulls. Paul suddenly realized where he'd seen a room like this before. At Salaman's house. "Still trying to escape me?" Paul turned and there, filling one window, was the unsmiling face of Salaman himself.

aul, this is not the end of your journey." And as Salaman's face disappeared, a huge wave smashed across the tower and swept through the room. Though Paul tried to hang on, he found himself being washed out and into the sea again. This time he sank down deeper and deeper, deeper than he'd ever been before, but as the sea cleared he made out far beneath him the rock he had seen in the globe and beside it the shining Mirrorstone. If he swam hard he might just reach it, though he was already deeper than three swimming pools on top of each other. With a gigantic effort he swam down and at last his feet touched the rock. Placing them firmly on its pitted surface, he edged slowly closer and closer until, stretching himself to his limit, his hand reached the stone.

He'd done it!

But as he looked into the stone there was no reflection of the shoals of fish and filtered sunlight around him. All he could see was a darkness deep and threatening. He turned and as he did so the rock moved beneath his feet. He felt himself sliding backwards along its rough black surface, struggling to keep his balance. Then, as he looked down, his heart went suddenly cold. He was staring not at the surface of a rock but into the center of an enormous eye!

The pupil of the eye widened, then narrowed, and Paul could see himself reflected in it, white and shaking with fear.

Gripping the Mirrorstone tightly, he flung himself away as the eyeball seemed to expand and grow red and angry. He looked behind him. The whole rock

was alive! It began slowly to uncoil itself into
something enormous and glistening and scaly.

    What had seemed to be solid stone parted
to reveal teeth as strong and hard as rock itself.
As the thing awoke it began to hiss and the water
all around swirled and frothed. Paul desperately
kicked upwards, heading for the surface.

    The creature's jagged claws shot out and
caught fast in his tunic. He twisted and kicked and writhed and
struggled. When he looked up, the surface of the sea seemed a
million miles away.

He felt himself sinking, his lungs bursting. But he *was* the best swimmer in the school and he gave one last mighty push, his tunic ripped and the claws of the rock creature slipped from him.

Paul shot to the surface and burst out of the water. He never knew fresh air could taste so good.

He tried to swim but he found he could hardly move. There was something stopping him.

He put his hand up to push against the unseen force.

He turned one way and then the other. Paul realized with a sinking heart that he was trapped.

He was surrounded by glass. And outside the glass was a face he recognized only too well.

Salaman screamed in triumph as he held high the crystal ball in which Paul squirmed and wriggled. "My plan has worked! Mary, I *am* a genius!" Mary could see Paul struggling and she knew he had little strength left.

"Let him go, please let him go!"

Salaman pushed her to one side.

"Not until I see the stone!" he cried. Paul clawed his way helplessly around the slippery sides of the globe.

"He'll die!" shouted Mary. "Send him back where you brought him from before it's too late!"

"Show me the stone!" Salaman screamed and Paul, with the last ounce of his strength, unclenched his fist and pressed the Mirrorstone to the side of the glass. But as Salaman stared into it the look of triumph drained from his face. What he saw in there was not the face of a genius. All he saw was a very old man whose face was lined and wrinkled as if he had lived a dozen lifetimes. He started back with a sharp cry of disappointment, and as he did so the globe slipped from his fingers and rolled onto the table.

ary!" shouted Salaman. "The Mirrorstone!"
But Mary did nothing.
The globe rolled the length of the table, halted
momentarily at the edge and, as Salaman leapt to save
it, toppled over and hit the ground with a tremendous
crash of splintering, shattering glass. Paul felt himself
hurtling through the air and a moment later he was lying in a heap
on his bathroom floor.

He lay there gasping for breath, his heart beating like a
sledgehammer. He heard the sound of a key in the door, and a light
went on in the hallway.

"Paul?"

Never had he been so happy to hear his mother's voice. He wanted to run to her but he hadn't the strength to move. He heard her footsteps cross the sitting room and at last she pushed open the bathroom door. She didn't seem nearly as pleased to see him as he was to see her. She stared open-mouthed first at the mirror and then at Paul.

"What *have* you been doing?" Paul looked down at the torn, bloodstained tunic Mary and Salaman had given him and he knew that no matter how much of the truth he told, he would never be believed.

"Only a dressing-up game," he mumbled.

"Dressing-up game!" She bent down and pulled him up. "Just look at you!" She turned him towards what was left of the mirror. And this time, when Paul smiled at his reflection, the face in the mirror smiled back.